Praise for *Kisses from Heaven*

"The history of God encounters with humankind began with Adam and Eve in the Garden of Eden and continues today. If you believe you have never had a God encounter, I beg to differ with you. You were afraid to admit it, but as you read these stories, you will discover yourself within them. The trip will be so enjoyable you will eagerly ask friends to join you."

—**David Craig**, Co-Senior Pastor, Life Church,
Sikeston, Missouri
Author, *My Supernatural Life*

"Challenging, enjoyable, and believable. These are three words that describe this wonderful book of real-life tales revealing how deeply the Lord involves Himself in our daily lives. I have known the Woodworths for many years and can attest to their willingness to do whatever Holy Spirit asks of them. Their faith carries the presence of God wherever they go."

—**Pastor Rick Kiddy**, Beauty for Ashes,
Mesa, Arizona

"Not only did Caleb and Emily teach me what a deep and powerful prayer life looks like, but they also stirred a longing in my heart to experience a mighty move of God in signs and wonders. Through their testimonies of courageous and simple obedience to the Lord's voice and prompting in their lives, they helped open my eyes to what an adventure the Christian life could be. Kisses from Heaven is a beautiful compilation of such adventures, and I pray they will stir your heart to seek after God's presence as well."

—**Pastor Hamilton Musser**, Cornerstone Church,
Bayview, Texas

"The Kisses from Heaven trilogy has been my life to live since the mid-1990s. So, who better to be a witness to its authenticity and of the primary author, Caleb, a man of integrity and lover of the Most High God. Even as His stories often astounded my husband and me, we are confident they will challenge, inspire, and bless you with the revelation of God's earnest desire to show Himself to those who love Him in magnificent ways we never thought possible. Now, Christian, read these tales, rejoice, and know beyond reason: 'He is alive.'"

—**Emily Anne Woodworth**, Caleb's Loving Wife and Daughter of the King

A TRILOGY OF
GOD'S STORIES

Kisses from Heaven

BOOK THREE

*Unique, Inexplicable, Extraordinary,
and Supernatural Tales from the
Heart of a Miraculous God*

"Publish His glorious deeds among the nations.
Tell everyone about the amazing things He does."
—Psalm 96:3, NLT

C. B. Caleb Woodworth, MD
with My Dear Wife and Co-author, Emily Woodworth

Kisses from Heaven: Unique, Inexplicable, Extraordinary, and Supernatural Tales from the Heart of a Miraculous God
A Trilogy of God's Stories, Book Three

Copyright ©2024 C. B. Caleb Woodworth, MD, with Emily Woodworth
ALL RIGHTS RESERVED

No part of this book may be reproduced, stored, or transmitted by any means—whether auditory, graphic, mechanical, or electronic—without written permission of both publisher and author, except in the case of brief excerpts used in critical articles and reviews. Unauthorized reproduction of any part of this work is illegal and is punishable by law..

Published by Face to Face Ministries

The cover was designed using assets by studio4rt from Freepik.com.
Book design by Inspire Books

Scripture quotations taken from the (NASB®) New American Standard Bible®, Copyright © 1960, 1971, 1973 by The Lockman Foundation. Used by permission. All rights reserved. Lockman.org.

Scripture quotations marked (NIV) are taken from the Holy Bible, New International Version®, NIV®. Copyright © 1973, 1978, 1984, 2011 by Biblica, Inc.™ Used by permission of Zondervan. All rights reserved worldwide. www.zondervan.comThe "NIV" and "New International Version" are trademarks registered in the United States Patent and Trademark Office by Biblica, Inc.™

Paperback ISBN: 979-8-9899945-6-4
Hardcover ISBN: 979-8-9899945-7-1
e-book ISBN: 979-8-9899945-8-8

Printed in the United States of America

Disclaimer: These true stories are seen as factual through the eyes of the one who lived and chronicled them, so are based on the author's experiences and opinions, expounded by his personal interpretations, and wide open to others good will observations. However, before we deliberate in love, dear one, it is wise to remember that a man with an experience is rarely at the mercy of a man with an argument. Maybe never here. Names and places may have been altered to protect the innocent.

Dedication

To Holy Spirit, without whom we get nothing done (John 15:5).

To my Proverbs 31 wife, Emily, without whose love, encouragement, and patience this work would still be the stuff of dreams (Prov. 18:22).

To every soul kissed by Heaven in this book who came back to give to God the glory due His name (1 John 4:19, Matt. 10:8b).

Contents

Dedication v
Acknowledgments ix
Preface xi
Introduction xv
Introduction from Emily xix

1	A Water Landing (1965) 1
2	Khe Sanh in the Rear Window (1967–1968) 14
3	Don't Be Like the Horse (1973) A Tale of Failed Revenge 27
4	The Hound of Heaven (1974) 39
5	Wolf Stories (1979-1997) 52
6	The Bushel of Corn (1980) 62
7	It Takes a Village (1982) 73
8	Making Friends (1982) 82
9	A Black Cloud (1983) 92
10	A Mid-Afternoon Snooze (1983) 101
11	In the Heart of Darkness (1984) 106
12	The Number Two Elevator (1984) 115
13	Catharsis in Creswell (1985) 122
14	Power of the Tongue (1985/1998) 134
15	Trashcan Man (1989) 141
16	The Romanian Shepherd (1991) 152
17	Hooked Up by Heaven (1997) 160
18	The Tangible Anointing (1998) 171

19	The Call (1998) 176
20	A Biblical Plague (2005) 182
21	No Stranger to Paradise (2007) 190
22	The Boat Keys (2008) 198
23	Tribute to Daisy (2011) 207

Afterthoughts 217
About the Authors 221

Acknowledgments

Captain Bill Chamberlin, an unknown "angel" aviator; Greg "Pappy" Boyington, an Air Force spotter pilot; Hijack and a coyote; Suzanne and Pastor Mac Wright; an old man who loved broken-down wolves; Charles Jr. and a lone timber wolf; Pastor Rob and a selfless gardener; Gig and Jillsey; a little Down syndrome boy and his folks; Pal Al Perna; Amy and her siblings; Canadian geese; turkey buzzards; Pastor Bob's and Tim's evangelical team; Melanie and her grateful father; an old huggable WWII veteran; a Filipino tenor and Emily; "dark and piercing eyes" and "trashcan man"; a Romanian shepherd; Pastors Minnie and Dewayne Faulk; an unknown pastor from Pensacola; an RV park postal clerk; Emily, the wee beasties, and the finger of God; Pastor Arnell Cadelina and son, Charles, and the Lord, Holy Spirit, and Daisy the dog; Emily (my faithful wife), Gary Jeter (encourager, computer scribe, and friend); and Beth Lottig of Inspire Books (our book coach and more).Thank you and bless all for participating in bringing the Lord glory due His name. For those "Flown West" (aviator lingo for having passed), give our love to Jesus.

Preface

Do you believe that inexplicable, extraordinary, and supernatural events are a part of Christian life in this present age? Do you accept that miracles and close encounters of a God kind are still in play today? Would you at least agree that Jesus stays intimately connected with His saints through day-to-day prayer, worship, and communication with Holy Spirit to reveal His will in ordinary human activity? If not so much, how about this? Would you consider that He uses heartwarming circumstances, near misses from disasters, happenstances in nature, and things we commonly call coincidence, serendipity, kismet, karma, chance, or luck to covertly manifest His personal interest and involvement in our lives? If not, save time and put this book away lest you struggle to receive what you read. But if you are the least bit curious or have the slightest inclination that maybe, just maybe, all the ongoing reports by millions of Bible-believing Christians throughout the world who insist that Jesus is alive and well on planet Earth and still working purposefully in the lives of His people may be true, then hold tight because you have epic tales coming your way.

Until two decades ago, we shared these God encounters with but two or three trustworthy friends. Then, unsolicited, Holy Spirit spoke up, asking these experiences to be passed along in a broader way. Obediently, over the next twenty years, they were chronicled in book form, which, with His agreement, I sensed, were to be dubbed "Kisses from Heaven: A Trilogy of God's Stories."

For my detractors, a history as a WWII child patriot, United States Naval aviator, Vietnam Marine Corps veteran, small-town medical doctor, larger-town clinic director, ordained pastor, long-term-short-term missionary, and restoration (inner healing) prayer minister for over thirty years will hold little sway. Instead, I will be evaluated from whatever doctrinal stance my readers embrace as either a true believer with the Lord glorified or pegged a liar, hyper-spiritual nutcase, or deceived by devils by today's not-so-easily-recognized body of Christ.

While defending myself by self-administered mental health evaluations (normal, you might argue, is merely a setting on one's dryer), impeccable references (less impressive, you might contend, if you exclude my mother and dog, both with Jesus), a fair share of Scripture documentation (one, you might refute, can find Scripture to support nearly anything), and a history of Christian service that might have made Mother Theresa proud (a frank pipedream, you might agree, but depending on what is in the pipe), this long-term literary work will be challenged by today's "miracles-are-not-for-today" folks in the body of Christ. Unbelief always whittles faith down to whatever size and shape fits the niche that unbelief has carved out for itself. Experiential spirituality then becomes a progressively smaller piece of the pie; check out the "Jesus Seminar" or the far liberal side of the church (no offense intended, dear ones) for ways to mitigate, minimize, or explain away the unique, inexplicable, extraordinary, and supernatural. Or if you have a chance, pick up the Jefferson Bible.

Now, to those of you not offended or prepared to put this book upon the shelf, I will unrepentantly say: "If you do not believe in the unique, inexplicable, extraordinary, or supernatural, it is because you do not read your Bible or have never experienced God in this way." You may be a devoted, well-intentioned, and faithful Christian, but, like Thomas the Doubter himself (who, you will agree, knew our Savior well), require Jesus to show you the beef before you believe. The reason you have not seen the beef is uncomplicated: You believe those unique, inexplicable, extraordinary, or supernatural experiences are not for today; this is not criticism, but it is reality. Truthfully, Thomas, this book may help you.

However, if you do believe that Jesus is unchangeable, the same yesterday, today, and forever (Heb. 13:8), are convinced that we are meant to do greater things than He did among us (John 14:12–14), or have tasted your own experiential "Kisses from Heaven," then you will enjoy this compendium of real-life events from an ordinary man's life.

These true tales may encourage and build your faith. They may cause you to laugh, cry, or force you to your knees while calling on the Lord for your own encounters or in grateful recognition that you, too, have enjoyed similar but unrecognized brushes with Holy Spirit throughout your walk. Mostly, I pray these experiences will draw you closer to Jesus, make Him more real and present in moment-to-moment ways, and open your heart to His ongoing divine, experiential, and life-changing involvement in your walk. Like all testimonies, those in this work look to bring others to Christ and us to greater faith, more gratitude, grander reverence, and but another way to glorify the Lord. And so should yours.

Finally, writing this real-life read came from unction and obedience but also because I know the Lord has, if we will open ourselves, believe, and draw near to Jesus (Jas. 4:8) during our everyday activities, a plethora of unsolicited, unplanned, unpetitioned, unique, inexplicable, extraordinary, and/or supernatural encounters with Himself. These experiences become arrows in our evangelical quivers, ready to give "legs" to the gospel by becoming attesting miracles (because any God encounter is a miracle) to Jesus as Lord, His Word, and a way to glorify the Father. All we need do is believe He wishes to commune with us, learn to recognize Him cloaked in the ordinary, and obey Him instantly, joyfully, and completely to receive our "Kisses from Heaven."

Introduction

This is a book of God Stories. That bold statement demands explanation. Who speaks for God? Not this man. So, let's try to define a God Story not by its content, for as we will see, each story speaks for itself, but by what criteria qualifies it to bear such a heady title. Is there a higher experience for a born-again Christian than to become a privileged moving part in a wondrous story created, choreographed, and christened by the Father, the only One who can guarantee Himself the glory He deserves? Let us see what it takes, at least from the eyes of this mere human.

God's Intimate Presence

God's intimate involvement defines a God Story. Remove Father's hand, and there is no story, at least not one worth telling. Test that statement; read a God Story. Then, remove all the elements in it that make it unique, inexplicable, extraordinary, or supernatural. The result? The story ends! It becomes an unfinished event, inconclusive and void of any meaning on Earth or glowing significance in Heaven. A God Story excluding God becomes a hollow collection of thoughts, words, and actions, a narrative with no divine worth or purpose.

God's Wondrous Character

A God Story always portrays the character and works of God as wondrous. What has happened in the story makes it difficult to describe or discuss without reaching beyond the ordinary and into the sublime. Applying uncertain or ill-defined words like luck, kismet, karma, serendipity, coincidence, or chance to explain a God Story only tarnishes the story's credibility and diminishes its meaning. Father's thumbprints, often hidden throughout a tale, are enough to confirm its place as a God Story.

God's Benevolent Intent

God Stories are uplifting, encouraging, edifying, or comforting for those both participating in the story or those listening to it further on as a testimony. God Stories leave no doubt as to Father's pristine character (proving who He is) and His infinite power (displaying what He does). Even more, they reinforce His loving intent toward us, which always supplies listeners with grateful hearts, elevated faith, and awe, if not worship for His inalterably benevolent heart and beneficent ways.

God's Lifelong Lessons

Lessons well learned remain as jewels mined from the residual of any passing God Story. Whether with knowledge gained relevant to a specific moment or wisdom applicable to life over the long haul, the Lord rarely transits our lives without teaching His tailored truth. All we need do is slow down and allow Holy Spirit to unwrap the truth waiting for us in any God Story, whether arising from our own or others' testimonies.

God's Glory Due His Name

A God Story preeminently exalts God for who He is, what He does, and only by way of a moment He considers worthy of His glory. So, what greater privilege for a Christian than to be invited to play a living role in a God Story where He is at His glorified best, the unabashed purpose is to bring Him glory due His name, becomes an inevitable unsolicited "Kiss from Heaven" for any believer taking a privileged part, and, finally, brings an unchangeable living testimony of God's majesty even to those of us participating vicariously.

Questions

Do you question God's desire to bring you a story for His glory? How can you be certain that you are ready to hear Him? Are you a waiter and listener with ears to hear? Are you ready to obey instantly, joyfully, and completely* when you do? Are you ready for God to intervene in your most mundane of daily events or in the middle of the most impossibly demanding and inconvenient of situations? Are you willing to drop everything at a moment's notice to have your life turned upside down by God interrupting you in the most uncomfortable, inflexible, or humiliating of ways? Are you then willing to deny yourself, pick up your cross, and follow Him? Are you willing to lay down your life for your friend? Are you willing to enter an inferno for making your decision to accompany Him at all costs? How about bearing accusations of irresponsibility for not being a Christian, being a Christian in name only, a sociopathic liar, a hyper-spiritual whacko, unhinged, or demon-possessed? Ready to lose friends? Good friends? Family? Close family? Church family? Face jealousy? Condemnation? Rejection? Abandonment? Persecution?

We need not go further, do we? But we could. And Jesus did. So, if you are not ready to follow Him down this narrow highway, faithfully keep doing what you are doing that pleases Him. Though all His highways are narrow, and but one leads to the Father, there are many paths through His Kingdom. If you are ready for a wilderness journey into another promised land of milk and honey, adventurous "Caleb," let Him know, be on the alert, keep your toothbrush on call, and your backpack packed. Then, prepare yourself for the most remarkable years of your life. Always be aware that God is no respecter of persons, impartial, and more than ready to deliver you a "Kiss from Heaven" as an arrow to your evangelical quiver as a testimony to God's glory.

Postscript

Throughout this tome's writings, you will come across dependable "Postscripts" designed to give Holy Spirit a chance to comment or the author (more often scribe) to enter his ten cents' worth. Then, occasional lighthearted tales may seem to fall outside the parameters of a God Story. I admit to considering such delights only after added thought, which you may consider adequate as a "Kiss from Heaven" as we do. Still, please honor these tales as God-given (meaning they are purposeful) and Heaven sent to serve as testimonies (1) to the goodness of God in the land of the living (Ps. 27:13), (2) to enable both Jesus, His gospel, and His words to become relevant to our times and believable as lights to a progressively darkening world, and (3) to equip individual Christians to carry unique, inexplicable, extraordinary, and supernatural testimonies to build faith for themselves, convince others, and prove the gospel as apostacy grows, churches close, and our Bible is outlawed. No one participating in a God Story will ever be the same, will commonly be ruined for the ordinary but equipped with a living testimony to build their own faith, will draw others to Christ, and will bring glory to the Father. I must ask, Christian, when our race is run, "Have we any greater reason for inhabiting God's green earth?"

* *Forever Ruined for the Ordinary*, Joy Dawson, 2001, Thomas Nelson.

Introduction from Emily

Living a life of Kisses from Heaven has been an adventure as the wife of a man who is obedient to the call of God, day or night, rain or shine, snow, or—you understand. My husband is a true servant of the Lord. When we started this journey twenty-seven years ago by marrying, leaving our nine-to-five jobs, selling our home, and moving into a small motor coach, it was, admittedly, a stretch for me. But what a marvelous stretch it became—and all because we dared lay down the things of this world, pick up the cross of Christ, and follow hard after Him.

We quickly became acutely aware of Holy Spirit's voice and His unspoken interactions with us as we continued to diligently seek and, soon it seemed, find Him everywhere we turned. Then, every glorious adventure was followed by another.

As you read this book, keep in mind such a lifestyle can be a tad unpredictable, if not chaotic, to say the least; although it has not always been easy, it has absolutely been fulfilling. Whether or not you choose to follow a path like ours, know that God is always with us, always speaking, and forever working. It is simply up to us to make a conscious effort to make ourselves available and aware of His purposeful laboring in our lives and the lives of those around us.

If we seek Him with all our hearts, He will soon be found, and all because He helps us get out of our own ways to make room for His.

A Water Landing (1965)

President Harry S. Truman, having constitutionally assumed the office as our nation's top executive with the premature death of President Franklin Delano Roosevelt on April 12, 1945, famously engraved on the annals of modern history, "The buck stops here." "Here," for President Harry, meant the desk he flew in the White House's Oval Office where, in August of that year, he was to make a pair of world-changing decisions to end four years of brutal war with the Japanese in the Pacific theater.

Following their president's order, the United States Army Air Force aircrew aboard the B-29 high-altitude Superfortress "Enola Gay" dropped the world's first military-grade nuclear weapon, a uranium bomb, "Little Man," from an altitude of 31,000 feet over the city of Hiroshima, an industrial center on mainland Japan. The first finished product of the Manhattan Project (a multi-year secret government effort to produce an atomic weapon in a keenly contested nuclear arms race with recently defeated Nazi Germany), "Little Man," a uranium weapon, would explode 1800 feet above Hiroshima to level that city on August 6, 1945. With the refusal by Japan to surrender following that initial attack, three days later, the president ordered a second mission, this with a 40 percent stronger plutonium bomb, "Fat Man," to ravage yet another industrial site and one-half the city of Nagasaki from the B-29 Superfortress "Bockscar." "Fat Man's" horror successfully brought about Japan's surrender, closure to WW II, a sigh of relief to the entire world on August 15, 1945, and the final signing documents officially ending the war on September 2, 1945. "The buck stops here" for today's peacetime civilian airline pilots is a cramped cockpit and avoiding becoming a considerably lesser bomb while approaching and leaving large cities several times a day for an entire work life.

"Okay," you ask, "where is the red threat or common denominator connecting President Truman's decision-making and that of today's commercial pilots?" Ask any aviator. It is headwork! I agree that the above history (with which all Americans should be familiar in these times of senseless and reckless nuclear threats) may seem a convoluted segue to the following discussion, but bear with me.

Headwork

Good headwork (making proper decisions and enforcing them expeditiously) by yesterday's president, although costing the lives of several hundred thousand Japanese civilians, saved millions more by ending the war. Today's professional pilots save similar numbers of citizen lives over extended careers by commonly making lifesaving decisions while conducting flights over our busy cities. Understandably, in the wake of today's aircraft accidents, pilots' decisions and their implementation often dominate investigations due to the plethora of strict regulations, rigid standards, and required procedures to which aircrews must adhere from approaching their aircraft before a flight until deplaning thereafter. Accident investigations focus on proving causes and preventing future repetitions. Formal boards take definitive procedural actions, which either end up helping vindicate pilots or assigning them pilot error. Even when an accident is unrelated to the pilot's decisions and actions, how the accident is managed also lands in the cockpit. So, pilots suffer double jeopardy since investigations must evaluate them as agents of both cause and ensuing mismanagement to walk away from an accident unscathed.

President Harry Truman and the desk he flew never suffered the same intense scrutiny, investigation, double jeopardy, or potential penalties for the Hiroshima and Nagasaki horrors as would the captain of a commercial aircraft crashing into a city today. The world in 1945 did suspect and accept that political, economic, financial, or other pressures helped short circuit the conventional way to win a war. Those reasons proved true but paled before the overarching reason that not using the bomb would incur countless more military lives on both sides, heavy civilian ones by the Japanese, and dropping a bomb (we had but two) in an uninhabited area to coerce Japan's surrender in advance would reduce our nuclear arsenal by 50 percent.

Discussions by two camps with opposing arguments have persisted nearly eighty years. Many have come from Monday morning quarterbacks who had opposed the ongoing carnage preceding the nuclear attacks but had not themselves participated in the South Pacific carnage. Countering the arguments condemning the bombing was a population sick of war, suffocating from an economy denying basic goods, distraught from losing loved ones to brutal enemies who had started the conflict, and the reality of our nation not having the finances nor the people's will to continue. Finally, the assaults on the two Japanese industrial sites were intended to spare the civilian population. Regrettably, neither our military leadership nor scientific community correctly calculated the human consequences nor how many of Hiroshima's and Nagasaki's citizens would be eliminated or crippled. Among the American people, who were grateful for victory, how we ultimately achieved it eventually met with those mixed reviews. Would all of us have had it another way, if possible? Of course. And to avoid a similar repeat in the future. By all means.

In Today's World of Aviation

Different kinds of unaddressed legal, political, economic, and financial pressures have arisen in today's world of aviation tragedies, which weigh on investigating boards to conduct their business free of those outside influences. The primary purpose for an investigation (discovering the reasons for an accident in order to prevent another) does not merely involve inspection of impersonal matters such as mechanical malfunctions, communication failures, or inclement weather but scrutinizes such areas as the pilot's headwork, responses, history of similar events, current states of both physical and mental health, stress levels, status of a variety of personal relationships, and the history of any medication use or substance abuse.

A negative outcome for the pilot in any area will have a serious impact on his or her future, professional life, career advancement, employment, financial, and family well-being. Understandably, discovering no obvious impersonal cause for an accident focuses attention upon the pilot. As the sole remaining piece of the puzzle, the pilot becomes a suspect simply by a diagnosis of exclusion. Regrettably, pilots will be in the running until other factors or the pilots themselves prove their own innocence. Why? Because the buck stops in the cockpit.

TWA Captain Bill Chamberlin

Difficult headwork scenarios put the investigative process to the test. There are double binds where no-win situations face pilots. It is here where we see headwork in the cockpit ascend to the forefront and create a dilemma for accident boards. A lifelong friend, Captain Bill Chamberlin, a former Air Force B-47 jock and thirty-year TWA veteran, had to defend himself before the FAA for entering a restricted area (in this case military airspace sometimes devoted to missilery) to avoid a towering thunderstorm late one night while in command of a flight carrying hundreds of passengers from New York City to Europe.

What a conundrum! He prevailed over time, but why the fuss? Would the Navy be conducting missile exercises at night amid a wild weather warning? No, but my friend broke an inflexible FAA rule and did not follow procedure by not avoiding that restricted area. His fate rested not with breaking that rule or disregarding a procedure so much as how well he evaluated his options: Did the "means" (entering the restricted area) justify the "end" (avoiding a thunderstorm that could have destroyed the aircraft and caused loss of life). The final determination depended on his headwork, and predictably, the buck stopped in the cockpit. Fortunately, despite being outside the letter of the law, the board exonerated him for this incident based on good headwork and a satisfactory outcome. Had the plane encountered a missile, we might have envisioned a different ending.

Sometimes, a board unearths no real impersonal cause or pilot error. That is a credit to the honest objectivity of a process willing to acknowledge its own fallibility. True accidents have no definable causes but "chance." Untainted objectivity, difficult during major investigations with imposing legal, political, economic, or financial pressures, often seems difficult with accident boards appearing to grasp at straws. The truth remains, as in any slice of life, that sometimes the truth itself is unavailable.

When complete, the entire reporting process is dependable and fair but highlights headwork in those unusual but very visible cases when pilots must stand alone to substantiate their innocence only because the process could not pin the tail on any other donkey. We are dealing with people (along with insurance money and lawyers) here, and assigning "chance" (without using the word) can appear, if not elusive, then suggesting incompetence of a board that may not even have found the donkey. Despite all those intense pressures, professional accident investigations are universally thorough, boards fair-minded and objective, while their conclusions supply valuable information to obviate future events.

US Airways Captain Chesley Sullenberger

The motion picture *Sully* details the controlled crash (and Hollywood's regrettable slanted portrayal of a lopsided turned humiliating but ultimately just investigation) of Capt. Chesley Sullenberger's heroic water landing (ditching) of US Airway's Flight 1549 on the Hudson River, where all on board were saved. Graphically illustrating a flight crew during the pressure-packed moments of a sudden in-flight emergency (multiple bird strikes engulfed by the engines followed by their failure), the accident challenged the National Transportation Safety Board investigating the mishap to maintain an initial tenacious but eventually yielded stance under the pressure of evolving facts presented by the flight crew and revelation by the board's own investigation. Considering how this board—under outside disparate pressures, evaluations reached by its own members, those of the flight officers themselves, and a narrative from a historically drama-driven press—evolved into as satisfactory an outcome imaginable is more than gratifying. What fair-minded American could be anything but proud of this "Cool Hand Luke" professional aviator who heroically saved the lives of passengers who could have easily been our own? Yet, for a time, the board would go against America's grain based on less than a forthcoming investigation until an open mind to the views, arguments, outstanding headwork, and proper decision making in the cockpit won Sully and his crew the day. A tough job righteously weathered by all.

Opining the above, with no actual experience as an accident investigator or accident board member, I was instead a military pilot and the subject of an accident investigation following the loss of a government aircraft. So, I hope you will allow me the license to comment from a place where the buck landed.

Marine Captain C.B. Woodworth

Squadron VMA 324, flying A4E Skyhawk single-pilot jet attack aircraft stationed aboard the USS Independence (CVA 62), was conducting exercises in the waters off Sicily in the fall of 1965. It was a day where you could see forever under bright blue skies and a dazzling warm sun. Looking to fulfill an in-flight refueling training requirement, I looked to rendezvous with a buddy-tanker, another A4E Skyhawk with a fuel store hung beneath the aircraft circling at altitude, to take on fuel. Approaching the drogue, a funnel-shaped basket attached to the end of a long hose extending from the tanker's "buddy store," I inserted my plane's refueling probe (projecting from the starboard side of the Skyhawk's fuselage below the cockpit and forward of the right intake) deep within the recesses of the "buddy store's" basket. Instantly, a later estimated 150 gallons of JP-4 jet fuel gushed from an invisible failed union between the probe and drogue. Carried by the airstream, the shapeless bolus of JP-4 flew toward but past the cockpit to disappear down the A-4E's gaping intake to surprise a waiting turbine within. Immediately deploying the speed brakes to separate the probe from the basket caused the geyser of fuel to stop. Simultaneously, the fire warning light on the Skyhawk's instrument panel blazed along with an alarm and distinct explosions aft of the cockpit. Securing the engine while deploying the emergency generator, I placed the Skyhawk, now without power, in a wings-level 250-knot descent to keep the aircraft flying.

 Enveloped within a smoke-filled cockpit while furiously transmitting the details of the emergency and our present position from the ship, the message proved correct but delivered by a voice terse, frenetic, and an octave higher than accustomed (a condition commonly described as "pucker factor" by aviators). Fortunately, the carrier received my location as eighteen miles from the ship on a specified radial (bearing from the ship). Despite the cloud of intensely irritating opaque smoke severely limiting my vision, I robotically regurgitated the required actions ingrained by years of repetitive practice responding to simulated emergency conditions, this one, "fire warning light and smoke in the cockpit."

As if riding Strangelove's bomb (due to the proximity of an onboard fire to the aircraft's main fuel tank) was not enough, without warning, the aircraft's stick moved violently starboard and forward, ripping itself from my hand, and even with 100 percent effort could not be convinced to change positions. With that move, the aircraft became uncontrollable due presumably to erosion of pressurized hydraulic lines by the fire. With the airspeed exceeding 250 knots, my altimeter rapidly unwound toward five thousand feet. The Skyhawk was on fire, unresponsive, out of control, and approaching the prescribed minimum altitude for ejection during an emergency under NATOPS (Naval Air Training Operations Systems) manual rules. As if the untenable situation was not enough, regulations alone made it time to leave this unresponsive burning bird.

Decision Time

Not prone to be heroic or argue with policy, while assuming a position as erect as possible under the auguring G-forces of the now-whirling dervish, I grasped the face curtain and pulled it forcefully over my flight helmet and partially across its polarized face shield to egress the cockpit. The ejection seat (powered by a substantial rocket) instantly roared up its rails (following an already jettisoned canopy) into space, tumbled once, and kicked me away as bladders (akin to car air bags) in the seat inflated. Before my prayer of "Lord, I hope this 'chute opens" ended, the ejection was complete, the tumble executed, the bladders had dispatched me into space, the parachute poofed overhead into an enormous white chrysanthemum ("Every good and perfect gift comes from above," Jas. 1:17), and believe it or not, all the above squeezed within but one and one-half seconds.

Looking aloft at the heavenly expanse of gently fluttering white canopy silhouetted against an intensely deep blue sky caused me to melt. Suspended by a few square feet of nylon four thousand feet above the water, I felt safer, more alive, and more peaceful than at any earlier moment in my life. The colors about were brighter, the air fresher and the panorama below (a shimmering azure mirror of sea secretly meeting a soft blue sky somewhere on an indistinguishable horizon) was unspeakably beautiful. In a windless descent toward a still sea under a warm sun and a full sail, who could wish for more?

Suddenly, disrupting this reverie, the unruly aircraft, trailing black smoke in what appeared a flat spin, spiraled into view thousands of feet below only to plunge like a giant gray rock into the smooth water, shattering its unbroken tranquility by displacing concentric rings of enormous waves from its point of impact. "Quite a convenient and usable bullseye" passed through my mind.

Lacking enough reference points to accurately figure out their altitude above smooth seas, disoriented aviators parachuting above flat water in World War II occasionally left their chutes early (to avoid being tangled in parachute shroud lines on water entry), only to rocket hundreds of feet to their deaths. So, I waited until my boots broke the water's surface to activate the quick-release fittings, safely freeing the parachute from my torso harness. Plunging feet below the water's surface, life vest inflated during the descent, brought me to the surface like a bobbing cork with time to watch the liberated chute settle gently into the sea a mere one hundred feet away. The bathtub-comfortable water was convincing enough to linger for minutes before climbing into the one-man raft automatically deployed and inflated from the parachute's seat pack during the descent. (That innocent delay while enjoying the water took on more significance when, the following evening, an A-6 Intruder went down into a school of sharks three miles off the USS Independence's bow.) Not a minute in the raft, a familiar sound of rotor blades announced the approaching "Angel" (the name given to the rescue helicopter assigned the ship's flight operations). Within minutes after being lifted to the chopper by a lanyard, the bird flew safely back to the carrier.

Hero or Goat

Not knowing what to expect, I knew this accident would negatively affect both the carrier air group's and our own squadron's safety records. Not a good thing. The skippers would not be pleased, so this Marine was understandably anxious about the potential ramifications surrounding the loss. Gratefully, there was considerable fanfare on the carrier's flight deck after disembarking the "Angel." The captain of the USS Independence, our squadron's skipper (it was his assigned aircraft now resting in Davy Jones's locker), and my squadron brothers were present to welcome their soaked mate unharmed. Taken to sick bay, examined by the flight surgeon, and then debriefed by the safety officer, this aviator was ready for a power nap.

The following morning, the air group's first launch found me flying Richard MacDonald's wing to the practice bombing range near Sigonella, Italy. Seems naval aviation has a policy to get the boy back on the horse that bucked him with considerable dispatch. That was altogether fine. It was a gorgeous day to be alive, safe, and sound in the wild blue yonder again.

Innocence by Default

The accident report took months to complete. Questioned briefly twice, those interrogations shed no new light on the board's investigation. Thorough examinations of drogues, baskets, and probes under various conditions to pinpoint a malfunction helped little. After all the board's material evidence proved inconclusive, my "headwork" was left standing alone, and the buck had once again stopped in the cockpit. The system confirmed the legitimacy of the process when it refused to attribute fault to equipment failure, procedures, or people. The board's finding: neither material cause nor pilot error assigned. "Chance," the villainous perpetrator of any true accident, was judged guilty without directly saying so in the exhaustive report. The Skyhawk was absolved posthumously while all that headwork in the cockpit received a Kiss from Heaven on our way toward breaking tomorrow's surly bonds of earth.

Postscript

If you ever encounter A-4E Skyhawk models produced in their later years of service (now long retired from active duty), you will note fuel probes redesigned to include a peculiar horizontal S-turn that placed the starboard intakes out of harm's way from any unexpected spillage during in-flight refueling. That change said this: Either mine or another aviator's similar experience was the backbreaker, provoking a change for safety's sake when aeronautical engineers saw the potential to lose further aircraft to its earlier design.

Proud to assume and adopt this change as the "Woodworth fuel probe modification" (a pipe dream, but who knows for sure) as the sole legacy* left my brother squadron mates and beloved Marine Corps when leaving for medical school at the end of my next tour of duty, would have to be enough. Honestly, I would have welcomed the opportunity to eject heroically during that upcoming time of combat to earn a Silver Star or Distinguished Flying Cross but ultimately had to concede that jumping out of a crippled bird to earn a fuel probe modification would have to do. It would prove more difficult to pin alongside one's medals on a formal mess dress, but then we all cannot be Medal of Honor Winner Pappy Boyington of Black Sheep Squadron fame. Incidentally, I met Pappy (Greg) when privileged to be his elderly mother's (Gracie Hallenbeck) doctor in Oregon. That Kiss from Heaven is a discussion for another day and quite a good one.

C. B. Caleb Woodworth, MD

One caution: remind us to leave the grand and great-grandkids at home when we gather to share Pappy's tales. To keep them historically correct, our conversation could get a little salty. Come to think of it, without exception, every one of the man's war stories was well-seasoned. Doubt that? Ask any of my five wide-eyed children, all under the age of fourteen at that history-making moment, or their apoplectic mother baptized into World War II Marine aviation jargon at our supper table during that memorable evening when Pappy** came to call. On second thought, maybe we should leave well enough alone.

* Perhaps we could add the God Story following this one to that legacy.

** We should add that Greg Boyington "flew west" in 1988, requiring us to reschedule our debrief with Pappy after we, too, have slipped the surly bonds of earth with no Marine left behind, I will prayerfully add.

QUESTION: Where is the Kiss from Heaven from this God Story?

ANSWER: Good headwork leads to good decisions, saving lives. Ask President Harry Truman and Airline Captains Bill Chamberlin and "Sully" Sullenberger. Ask me as well. Asking for Medal of Honor Winner Pappy Boyington's decisions that defined his twenty-eight victories in and around World War II might take a little more time and a saltshaker or two. The Lord's headwork has always led to good decisions saving lives, which did not include His own. Sometimes, no good deed goes unpunished, saith my son, the lawyer. Jesus, however, insisted that no greater love has a man than he lay down his life for his friend (John 15:13). Who saw that contradiction coming? With it, many began to question the soundness of the Lord's headwork and His decisions. Many humans still do. Then again, 2,500,000,000 Christians, a third of our globe's population, happily do not. Now, there's a Kiss from Heaven for you. In this story, maybe that "poof" comes in a close second.

Khe Sanh in the Rear Window (1967–1968)

Khe Sanh, portrayed earlier as "an obscure little plateau in the rugged northwest corner of South Vietnam" by American forces Commander General William Westmoreland* (COMACV), purportedly became the worst military defeat suffered by US troops in the entire Vietnam conflict. If we look closely, it was not so much a defeat as a difficult holding action, which ended with a hard-earned Marine victory and troops walking away unhindered. In the end, the base was dismantled and plowed under by Westmoreland's replacement, General Creighton Abrams, to render it useless to the North Vietnamese forces, Peoples' Army of Vietnam (PAVN) and, regrettably, our own.

Khe Sanh: The Beginning of an End

Defending Khe Sanh in a battle against a full PAVN division (20,000-plus troops or more) led by capable General Vo Nguyen Giap had required more American infantry struggling elsewhere during the widespread Tet offensive. As an unexpected plus, that gallant defensive stand tied up Giap's division from further planned support of wider spread Tet objectives during the same period. Regrettably, the combined loss of American life from the battle for Khe Sanh (January 21–July 9, 1968), significant casualties sustained during military victories during the Tet offensive (January 2–September 23, 1968), and, later, a valiant but costly Hamburger Hill win (May 13–20, 1969) were viewed not as celebratory military actions by America's civilian home front but instead ended as political and psychological catastrophes.

Due to pressure from the US domestic community, a progressively negative press, and countless anti-war student demonstrations, President Lyndon Johnson, in a vainglorious attempt to save his embattled presidency in the election year of 1968, chose to adopt a policy of "Vietnamization" (pacification) throughout South Vietnam. Unfortunately, the ill-prepared South Vietnamese ARVN (Army of the Republic of Vietnam) was delegated the hopeless task of waging its own battles without American help, which eventually led to collapse of the allied cause. Like a surgeon's technique, which succeeds but the patient dies, Vietnamization was properly executed except by our ARVN ally, who had been too long corrupt and dependent upon the United States to overcome its well-entrenched and determined communist adversary. So, in the same election year of 1968, when the president was running for cover, the politicians joined in to mollify their fed-up constituencies over troop losses in country and a hated draft at home by supporting their embattled president in pacifying the enemy on the warfront. Then, making matters worse, Commander-(thought coward)-in-Chief Johnson abdicated that failed role by dropping his aspirations for re-election; the Secretary of Defense MacNamara similarly fled his post filled with "disillusionment" over a war lacking progress (due largely to his meddling decisions), and the oft-politically shackled field commander Westmoreland was handcuffed by a political rotation into a new billet as Army Chief of Staff. So, the above struck an eventual death knell to the United States' attempts to win the conflict, opened the door to years of de-escalation, and led to an eventual failure to keep communism from South Vietnam and beyond, which allegedly was America's primary reason for being there. Those prospering American big military weapons industrialists might have quietly disagreed with that assumption.

Khe Sanh: Going a Little Deeper

Established as a US Army Signal Corps Observation Post in 1962, the Khe Sanh plateau gradually blossomed into an airbase and the strategic anchor for I Corps, the five northernmost provinces in South Vietnam pressing against the DMZ (Demilitarized Zone) to the north and the country of Laos, sheltering the Ho Chi Minh trail twenty-five miles to the west. With the departure of the Signal Corps, 6,000 United States Marines had become both Khe Sanh's village and the base's primary defenders while continuing to covertly observe the southern movement of North Vietnamese supplies and weapons of war along the nearby Ho Chi Minh trail in Laos. General Westmoreland's grander vision saw Khe Sanh as the primary point to launch a massive assault into Laos to "cut the trail," cripple North Vietnam's major western supply route to the south, and quickly eradicate an essential lifeline. As mentioned, President Lyndon Johnson, who was up for re-election but plagued by a citizenry severely divided over the country's growing involvement in Vietnam, was in no way willing to self-destruct his re-election chances by expanding America's presence into another sovereign land. This self-serving political decision nipped Westmoreland's strategy in the bud and abolished the most promising option to quickly limit the conflict, i.e., cutting the trail.

The Amazing Ho Chi Minh Trail

Early on the trail was an elaborate system of nearly twelve thousand miles of mountain pathways and jungle rivers, which enabled Hanoi, by way of Laos and then Cambodia, to extend over twenty-three routes east into South Vietnam to supply imbedded North Vietnamese army and Viet Cong insurgents. A masterful engineering feat, its miles were clandestine and hidden among heavy three-level jungle foliage. Tunnels and underground bases along the way housed supply depots, command posts, feeding stations, personnel staging areas, and hospitals cleverly concealed from reconnaissance efforts by the US and ARVN forces. From the beginning, footpaths were occupied with citizens carrying one-hundred-pound packs (often from Hanoi to Saigon), re-enforced bicycles pushed along loaded with five-hundred-pounds of supplies, and pack animals (occasionally elephants) heavy-laden with the necessities of war.

Over the years, these primitive trails morphed (with the help of Russian, Chinese, and North Korean engineers) into eighteen feet wide asphalt highways lined with six-wheeled-trucks carrying military and medical supplies, food, and troops. Much travel was done at night by dimming vehicles' headlights, which, traveling at twenty miles per hour, would cover up to seventy-five miles before daylight. Over twenty thousand tons of weapons and goods per month traveled the trail maintained by up to one hundred thousand workers.

It is estimated that between one and two million people traveled back and forth over the Ho Chi Minh trail during the war years. Both sides agreed that whichever nation controlled the trail would decide the war's outcome. All attempts by the allies to cut the trail failed, including delivering twice the tonnage of bombs used by the United States and its allies during World War II. The Ho Chi Minh trail, one American general officer candidly remarked, was less a road than a state of mind.

Cutting the Trail

Now, the only known arm of the Ho Chi Minh trail wide enough to observe an attack, of which I was aware, ran through the A Shau valley. Into it, a supply-laden arm emerged from the main body of the trail in Laos, across the Laotian border into South Vietnam, through the valley, and on to east coast cities of Hue and Danang on the South China Sea. The A Shau was a twenty-five-mile long, one-mile-wide, open stretch guarded on either side by up to five thousand feet of heavily defended mountains.

So, let's be clear up front: Cutting the trail (a living fantasy among military planners for years) as it ran through the A Shau valley would be less like cutting the head off a snake than the tentacle from a squid (apologies to my Navy brothers), which, as we all know, may regenerate with ease. Still, there was I, a Marine aviator assigned to a four-plane flight as a part of today's mission, "Operation Tentacle." (Well, I cannot recall the true name, but does it matter?) With four A-4E Skyhawk aircraft configured with one seven-hundred-fifty-pound bomb beneath each wing and another two thousand-pounder on centerline, our mission, on that dreary monsoon season morning, was to "cut the trail" as it emerged as a tentacle from Laos into the A Shau valley with the surrounding mountainsides simultaneously bristling like porcupines with fifty-caliber tracers.

Below the fireworks in the flatlands lay a highway meandering alongside a river where neither means of transportation showed any activity. Our orders were to make this visit short and bomb the river from an altitude above the highest peak using a sixty-degree dive angle to avoid the porcupines. You might question: to what purpose is bombing a river? Well, to my best recollection, with high water in the basin following monsoon rains, our mission was intended to flood the A Shau by damming it like a big beaver to cut off movement of supplies, weapons, and troops along this section of the trail. The following morning, we repeated the mission only to be greeted from below by multiple enormous circular bomb-created lakes dotting the landscape, many giant muddy puddles carefully circumscribed by a pristine new road laid down overnight by the North Vietnamese.

This mission helped wrap up Operation Tentacle, and for good reason—what became a mere overnight inconvenience to the North Vietnamese highway department risked too many American pilots' lives and aircraft and cost our taxpayers way more than a mere pittance in useless bombing. Also, we aviators had long ago learned our enemy would adjust his defenses and have an effective welcoming committee were we to attempt an additional day's attack. A third run by aircraft from the same direction was already well known to render an aviator as vulnerable as the third soldier on a match in World War One. So, it was a relief to be notified this operation was shelved, although, to be honest, any jet jockey experiencing the nose of his aircraft pitching from a sixty-degree dive angle to twenty degrees above the horizon a tenth of a second after shedding 3400 pounds of ordinance would always be a memorable high-G carnival ride worth repeating under friendlier circumstances.

Mission Impossible: The Beginning

Not long after those A Shau flights, we were called to Khe Sanh, scarce miles north of those prickly hillsides, for a support mission. Weren't we grateful to see our birds limited to a manageable full load of five-hundred-pound bombs this time around. Still, it was Khe Sanh, maybe even the valley again, and a last-minute, unscheduled flight. That meant someone was in trouble, and live fire would be today's main event. Launching into an uncloudy sky was a good omen; it is always a plus to unmistakably see the target. How crucial that pristine crystal-clear sky would soon become to this aviator was well beyond his finest fantasies. Climbing out, the flight leader asked each aircraft to check in by radio. Darn it; I had lost my transmitter, and that would mean a no-go. Moving toward the leader while simultaneously tapping my mask and giving a thumbs down indicated my inability to transmit. He acknowledged the signal and instructed me to remain in orbit until the flight returned from Khe Sanh to retrieve my aircraft. As the rest of the flight left, I moved east toward the South China Sea, prepared to carve out an oversized circle at 10,000 feet for the next hour. It would be a lie to say I was not profoundly disappointed. Missing the opportunity to make a difference, save Marine lives, and do what Naval aviators are trained for (i.e., combat) stunk up what had been a promising day. I spent the first ten minutes auguring above a similar-sized circular blue patch of South China seawater. No other military aircraft were in sight. Only a pockmarked highway leaving North Vietnam, often the target of American high-altitude radar-controlled strikes after dark, was visible to the northwest.

An Emergency Transmission

My mind was roaming somewhere else when the Skyhawk's radio exploded to bring it back. An intense male voice, maybe half an octave high and brimming with a mixture of excitement and concern, was repeatedly blaring the same message over the guard channel, a frequency restricted to formal emergencies. After identifying himself as an Air Force reconnaissance (spotter) aircraft flying at an altitude of 2,000 feet eighty miles north of the DMZ on the coast of the South China Sea came this bone chiller, "SAM site in the open, SAM site in the open." (SAM 3 missiles, the latest Russian surface-to-air weapons recently reported in the DMZ, were nasty and, it is noteworthy, to be avoided at all costs.)

No problem for this aviator. Marines were restricted to flights south of the DMZ (a mile or two to the north of my present position), so I was no candidate to help the spotter in airspace assigned by the Air Force to the north. How frustrating was that? Here I was, ten minutes from helping a fellow aviator in a desperate and dangerous situation, whose own frustration was now flooding the airwaves while describing a prime enemy target wide open on the beach.

Kisses from Heaven, Book Three

Don't you know I was soon in an impossible, intense personal debate with myself. What an untenable situation for a Marine. Taught to obey without question and acutely aware that Air Force target was off-limits, the spotter's desperate calls for help kept convicting me as a fellow American fighting man for even hesitating a moment to help a comrade facing significant danger in that tiny defenseless spotter plane to complete his mission.

A Moral Struggle

Whoa, without warning, a powerful unction** (like many that would come from Holy Spirit as the years passed) rose in me to lay aside the fear of consequence and do the upright thing. It was so easy. No question or hesitation lingered. Time to go. Impetuously jamming the throttle full forward while pulling the aircraft due north along the coast, the die was cast, today's Rubicon crossed, and there was no heading back.

Well, easy did not last long. Don't you know my mind was working faster than that Skyhawk speeding over the ground at five hundred knots. First came the supporting arguments; after all, we were more than prepared with a full load of ordinance, which would need jettisoning before we landed anyway. Then, this was an opportunity to make a difference. We might save lives in that spotter plane today, but to be sure, other combat aircraft in the days following. Hey, the target was a vicious SAM site. Then came the opposition: "What are you doing? You are in direct disobedience of an order. The North is off-limits. This is not you. You have never even considered such a defiant act."

Then the pro: "Captain, that spotter plane is giving you permission to respond, even begging you to help. You are an essential in this mission. Just get it done." Followed by the con: "Yes," came the reply, "but you are asking for a court-martial for this craziness. What about your future? And what about your skipper's? He is a deliberate man and a rule keeper, not a take-no-prisoners kind of Marine. He will take the brunt of this and does not deserve it. What a mess you are creating to even think of this action." Then another rebuttal: "How many servicemen have chosen the high ground to sacrifice when faced with tough decisions like this? How many have gone outside artificial boundaries to serve a higher cause than self?"

Conniving While Driving

Then, almost as another epiphany, I saw the solution to this moral dilemma was right in front of us. Maybe it was not entirely forthright, but at least we could complete this mission in a way only the enemy would be hurt. Flying at top speed to the target, we would drop the ordinance as directed by the spotter and race back before our original flight returned from Khe Sanh. But what about the absent bombs? Everyone would assume the ordinance had been dropped over the water to save fuel and prepare for a required ordinance-free landing. Then, I had only to say nothing to anyone, and it would always remain an unsolvable mystery. One necessary final piece of the puzzle would be to stay anonymous to the pilots in the spotter plane. That could be done by departing altitude into a high-speed dive to pass the Air Force from the south, fifty feet east, and twenty feet above (to keep that little plane out of our jet wash). Then, when clear, executing a split-second, high-G, steep climbing turn west toward the beach and hopefully into the sun clear of the spotter aircraft (having gained the pilot's attention but denied a visual of the Skyhawk's tail numbers), would leave only the plane's tail pipe gathering distance between us. Finally, entering a sixty-degree dive above a surprised enemy, the ordinance would be delivered on target as we vanished to the south.

Well, we startled the Air Force, who, with great cheer and instant relief, gave directions, entered our attack against an easily identified pristine SAM site on the beach, avoided a load of flack two hundred feet starboard from a not-so-surprised enemy (but gratefully saw no missiles underway), spread the bombs along what looked to be launching pads and buildings below (the play-by-play reported by a now-delirious spotter pilot), full-powered our way south, joined up with today's original flight, and arrived home with time to push a few papers as the squadron's administrative officer before the workday was over (which was never in that place). It would end up a kind of Clark Kent to Superman to Clark Kent move with no one the wiser... I hoped.

Mission Impossible: The Aftermath

Predictably, the following week, I was approached in the ready room by our safety officer, who advised that Air Force pilots had visited our squadron spaces to ask if the Marines were aware of a peculiar event where an unidentified aircraft aided an Air Force spotter plane by destroying a newly erected SAM site on the beach along the South China Sea eighty miles north of the DMZ. Nobody knew a thing, he reported. Thankfully, I was never asked by that Marine brother if I had any part in or knowledge of the whole shebang. And don't you suppose somebody on that flight had connected the dots? But not a word. Sometimes, I wonder if the Lord didn't choreograph that day on the South China Sea when we were privileged to rid this cruel world of an enemy SAM site to save not just a few aircraft and airmen from missile strikes during the soon-to-materialize Tet offensive of 1968. In a way, it makes me feel like an early partner in that difficult battle, but from a distance. I would be in Japan, having completed my tour of duty, and on the way stateside as the only clear Kiss from Heaven in this story.

Postscript

The skipper of a squadron and his administrative officer spend hours pushing papers back and forth. My VMA 223 Bulldog's commanding officer and I were no different. I sensed a little distance after my trip north of the DMZ. Now, that could have been my regret for risking his future or maybe his regret that I could not trust him with mine. Until today, this heretofore unconfessed and ambivalent time in my service as a Marine aviator will always stand as a testimony that hard decisions may occasionally break the rules as a part of life, but righteous motives can make them livable. "Do not judge according to appearance, but judge with righteous judgment" (John 7:24). When it was over, had the Air Force considered our action worthy of a medal while the Marine Corps simultaneously deliberated a court-martial? Who knew? So go the yin and yang of life. Sometimes, we cannot get the one without the other. This turned out to be one of those rare moments where feelings of shame (for defying an order, risking my skipper's career, and being unwilling to stand for my decision) and self-respect (for coming to that Air Force spotter's aid and his mission to eliminate an immediate and long-term risk for all allied pilots) had to share the same hiding place. What became the solution to this moral conundrum? An oft-quoted proverb (when paraphrased): "Even a fool, when he keeps silent, is considered wise" (Prov. 17:28). A rather uncourageous stance by itself, wouldn't you say? Well, at least until now.

Our short story shared here ends in 1968, but the Vietnam conflict continued into 1975. Much information regarding those years suggests the war was lost not by major American military operations (which, ironically, before its conclusion, were covertly carried out within Laotian and Cambodian sections of the Ho Chi Minh trail) but by politicians meddling with military plans and operations. If true, then 50,000 innocent American lives were squandered not so much in the brave fields of battle but in the cowardly halls of government. God bless the Vietnam veterans whose lives were sacrificed upon the altar of political expediency and a long-overdue repentant America. Decades later, it came to honor those reluctant warriors, whose true enemy was never hidden in the just jungles of Vietnam where the best of men could live to fight another day but within the vile political and media cesspools of our nation's capital, where even the best of men too often go, die to their souls, and fight no more. Painfully said but tragically true.*** Rest in honor, my warrior brothers. You did not lose the war. Through Vietnamization, America's politicians forced you to lay down your arms, and the South Vietnamese army could not finish the fight. You proudly did your job and deserved better both abroad and at home . . . and still do.

*My daughter Melanie and I needed a ride, so General Westmoreland welcomed us aboard his privately chartered boat leaving Manila to Corregidor with a group of his military friends in the mid-1980s. The general seemed a friendly, considerate, and "regular guy," well-versed in conversation and humor, but not the kind of a man you might expect to run a war—which, ironically, history has since strongly suggested he didn't.

**Here, the word unction is seen as a settled urgency leading to a willingness to take a higher road, often in the face of legitimate opposition. To a born-again Christian-in-waiting, it may have simply been obeying Holy Spirit without so knowing.

***Curiously, in a backhanded way, it seems the Vietnam conflict did meet America's goal to stop communism from spreading through Cambodia, Thailand, and further into Malaysia, Indonesia, and the Philippines. Here's how: A unified communist Vietnam entered Cambodia in 1978 to eradicate the infamous killing fields and overthrow the brutal Pol Pot-led communist Khmer Rouge government. After seizing control, under years of mounting world pressure, the Vietnamese surrendered power and withdrew in 1989. How ironic; without knowing, the same Vietnam communists we sought to prevent spreading their ideology throughout Asia were the identical people who ultimately brought that objective about and, rightfully so, raised the painful question to all critical thinkers in America as to whether the Vietnam conflict had been necessary in the least.

QUESTION: Where is the Kiss from Heaven from this God Story?

ANSWER: Have you ever been in a moral dilemma where (1) right seems wrong and wrong seems right, (2) struggle to determine under the circumstances which is which, (3) wonder if both decisions are equally right or wrong, (4) one is Heaven sent from the Commander-in-Chief and the other from headquarters and the commandant of the Marine Corps, and (5) nearly sixty years later cannot honestly answer those questions without reservation, qualification, clarification, and a lot more word salad. I'll let you mull that one over. In my "retrospectascope," it is what it is, water under the bridge or spilled milk... both or neither. Happily, most of my ambivalence surrounding this half-century-old moral conundrum now peacefully co-exists alongside the few remaining shards of others-centered decisiveness I still hold dear from that mission. Knowing that Air Force spotter pilot and a bunch of other Marine troopers and aircrew were blessed to live safer lives before, during, and after the upcoming Tet offensive (1968) by doing the right (or wrong) thing that day has had to be my Kiss from Heaven here. Well, not exposing my skipper has been a bonus... for the both of us when you understand the gravity of military gravitas.

Don't Be Like the Horse (1973)
A Tale of Failed Revenge

If you live or have ever lived in rural America with children, particularly the female variety, there is a distinct possibility a "backyard horse" will be in your family's future. If this horse is not in the cards dealt you, then don't hold 'em but fold 'em, thank Jesus for His mercy, continue your blessed way, and never look back. If, however, your unfulfilled lifelong dream is to own a "backyard horse" as a family companion, would you, for your loved ones' safety, first consider adopting a gentler and more lovable alternative? A cuddly orphaned hyena or, if appendages on your pet are not essential, a tenderhearted black mamba might work. Both are unique attention getters in the neighborhood and, as the mother of all benefits, you need not room, groom, saddle, or straddle either.

If a backyard horse as the road to family togetherness looms unavoidable, to help introduce each of your loved ones to and prepare for the unavoidable, take a small family trip in a large family-size barrel over, say, Niagara Falls? Try the American side first, unless you contemplate adopting two horses (you know, so they have "companionship" and do not get "lonely"); then, simply save time by making a beeline to the more challenging Canadian falls. Know, however, that you will graphically expose your character by subjecting those under your care to such unavoidable peril. No, no, not to Niagara Falls, friend... to the "backyard horse"! Know that the backyard horse is a novel breed. "How so?" you ask.

Ah, let me summarize: The backyard horse is an entitled horse who rarely does what you want when you want but instead does what it wants when it wants within the confines of the feed room, where it faces multiple outstanding and incontestable warrants for breaking and entering alongside the unmitigated sin of gluttony. As we speak, flashbacks, bipolar waves of sweet nostalgia suddenly challenged by tsunamis of stark panic arising from years of backyard horse terrorism flood my mind. Are we talking paradoxes here? Yes, but not just run-of-the-mill paradox but pharmaceutical-grade paradox on steroids for those who have lived through the chilling saga of "my life and times with a backyard horse."

More of the Same

Understandably, during this brief soliloquy, I have offended a sizable percentage of the small percentage of the horsey female readers still with us. "That is so unfair. Our horse is one of the family. She is so sweet." I might query, my dear fräuleins, does that ring true because your badgered husband and enslaved children are the ones who (1) eternally muck the barn, (2) ceaselessly replace the cribbed corral fencing, (3) unwillingly answer the neighbor's phone call at 2:00 a.m. about "your horse" in "their garden," (4) tenaciously retrieve the same horse after a three-hour marathon chase in the sole monsoon-like downpour in San Diego county in the last twenty years, (5) repeatedly rescue one of your panicked children from the back of that peevish mare with PMS, (6) time after time replace the crushed PVC sprinkler heads following another "great escape," and, last but not least, (7) faithfully repair the unhinged door to the oft-pilfered and often-emptied feed room at least one hundred times a month? (Okay, I am using a little literary license for effect, but don't you think I deserve it?)

It is now necessary to address the spiraling negativity from the few indignant ladies who proudly report they actually suffer through the above. In my (in)considerate opinion, dear ones, either you are taking credit for chores accomplished by an obedient slave (I remind you that owning a slave is mostly against the law nowadays), have a closeted stay-at-home significant other whose dark past you have threatened to expose as an "encouragement" to oversee your domestic world, or you suffer from a severe atypical form of obsessive-compulsive disorder, which never ("I need to groom the horse"), never ("I need to worm the horse"), never ("I need to shoe the horse"), never ("I need to train the horse"), never ("I need to ride the horse") ever lets you stop your eternal striving and driving behavior in anything—and I mean anything—you do.

"How," you demand, "does this misogynist have the unmitigated gall to say all these unchristian, outlandish, intolerant, sexist, and mean-spirited things?" Honestly, it is easy. Here is the truth: As a "backyard horse" owner (truly a misnomer of pure delusion because nobody "owns" a horse), you must eventually choose between your mental health and that "possessed" equine. It is out of the question to achieve both if you wish to avoid electroconvulsive therapy (ECT) or, at the very least, high-dose Prozac and a daily session with Dr. Phil. Now, please, despite your escalating anger (which, I humbly submit, could use a little work also), would you just settle down, be a tad less intolerant (your word of choice here, not mine), and let me share true life events to support my position, untenable as it may seem to thee?

The Happy Arrival of Hijack

What is in a name? Considering what that "backyard horse" did (You are catching my drift right out of the gate, aren't you?), let us begin here. Hijack was an apt epithet for the powerful two-year-old, seventeen-hands-high, giant brown saddle-bred gelding with an aquiline nose challenging Caesar's who came to live with us on a lovely summer day I thought nothing could ruin. As is commonly the case, I was wrong. Imposing, if not a little scary, he turned out to be a "green-broke" steed, which my wife and daughters found advertised in the "Penny Saver" or another thrifty shopper throwaway of similar ilk. He arrived that fateful day in the early 1970s, along with Duchess, a seven-year-old well-trained but severely cranky and hormonal Palomino mare, to our one-quarter acre corral built with loving anticipation, which bordered the rolling 300-acre Daley Ranch in North San Diego County.

Our little homestead, along with scores of other houses on Hilltop Circle (which was a perfect square, but then we were in California), pushed its way into ranch land whose owner had generously allowed us as "Hilltopper horse owners" unlimited access. Can you imagine an owner allowing that leeway in today's litigious society? It was the best of all worlds for any enthusiastic "backyard horse" owner, except that it fell upon not-so-enthusiastic-me (who had ridden only sparingly over the years) to gentle the Hijack monster for the children. Regrettably, with subtle ego tweaking applied by the female side of the family, I became, in time, overconfident, a tad arrogant, deceived, and foolishly eager to tame the beast. "Bring him on," I thought with no shred of common sense or humility, "this should be a fine contest of wills."

Now, whether trumped by my lack of caution, common sense, present pride, the entire trifecta or seduced by the big brown boy's (generally) obedient ways and (most of the time) gentle nature with the children, there came a moment when bewitched by my de-escalating sense of ambivalence, I came to trust the behemoth (horse rule numbers 1–10: never, but never, trust a "behemoth").

From that day forward, we began our rather-one-sided relationship. His boundless energy was only partly spent by sprinting up an entire one-half mile, fifteen-degree slope leading to the more remote parts of our neighbor's ranch. Even with that effort, the horse barely broke a sweat and, once at the summit, would take any opportunity to engage in a pickup game of tag with a member of our local pack of coyotes caught unawares and snoozing under a couple shade trees in the late afternoon sun. It was nothing for Hijack to effortlessly gallop for miles while shadowing a shifty coyote who, frantically looking over its shoulders, darted this way and that to avoid the big brown boy's thunderous pursuit. The horse never tried to injure his prey but kept a couple horse lengths behind, enthusiastically enjoying the tail chase, which, in looking back, was merely ecstasy over the coyote's mounting distress. For a time, I mistakenly took this behavior as mildly considerate and that of a bully in remission.

The Riding and Not-So-Much Riding of Hijack

One sun-drenched Saturday, like every glorious afternoon in North San Diego County, with me aboard the big brown boy, we flew once again to the top of that monster hill in search of his slumbering quarry. Quickly engaged, Hijack remained intently focused on tail-chasing a shifty but rightfully nervous coyote in rare athletic form and busy using all his best tactical avoidance maneuvers to lose the giant nemesis in full pursuit. At one point, the contest was even-steven when, in the blink of an eye and one unexpected deft move later, the coyote vanished over the crest of a hill as his panting pursuer was closing the gap.

Now, I lacked the sense not to allow Hijack the following latitude. Running an untested horse downhill is so unwise, but I was so enjoying the boy so enjoying himself. Alas, throwing caution to the wind, along with my few remaining shards of horse sense, over the crest we flew in a horse and rider swan dive right out of *The Man from Snowy River*. Now, I remain uncertain of how Big Brown performed what followed, being airborne as we were, but with the athletic prowess of an Olympic gymnast draped in gold, Hijack's hindquarters elevated themselves halfway up the face of K2, all the while shaking like a wet

Labrador fresh from the millpond. During this brief unsettling moment, I unwittingly became a smaller version of a NASA space vehicle with, sadly, no protocol for a safe re-entry.

To this day, the launch remains memorable but, mercifully, not the re-entry. What remains clear, after regaining a facsimile of consciousness, was lying flat on my face, sampling a mouth full of used pasture grass. No need to elaborate further. Encountering a quiet panic (another cryptic "backyard horse" related oxymoron), I carefully assessed each body part designed to move voluntarily from my toes north. Aside from one severely deformed, painful, non-functioning, and obviously fractured left wrist, all parts were cheerfully in working order. Rolling over to check my surroundings, I saw that giant brown ingrate obliviously grazing twenty feet downwind on the same grass I was now plucking one-handed from my gratefully intact teeth.

Narrowed with suspicion, my eyes scrutinized this gentle giant picture, concluding that it was merely a wily facade masking cunning horseflesh housing a severely duplicitous nature. (Have I mentioned the creeping paranoia that gradually overtakes the backyard horse owner after repeated betrayals?)

Severed right rein still gripped tightly in the only remaining functional hand left, I struggled to my feet, spewing used shards of pasture grass along the way, and stumbled toward the beast with that wounded left wrist pressed firmly to my belly. Goliath ignored David. Talk about salt in the wound of disrespect. "Very undisciplined piece of horseflesh, to be sure," I growled. We would tend to that later, but for the moment, it was "Hi, ho, Silver, away" to the orthopedic clinic. Jury-rigging the rein in place and struggling aboard, the horse wisely inched his way back down that long hill where I set forth on a one-handed drive to the naval hospital at Balboa, forty-five minutes to the south.

Kisses from Heaven, Book Three

The Riding and Not So Much Riding of Hijack II

While returning home from the orthopedic clinic hours later, left arm encased in a long arm plaster cast (which ran all the way from my left hand to a not-so-nearby left shoulder while pausing only briefly to make a permanent right-angle turn at the elbow), the closer to home I got, the more I ruminated on the horse's behavior and the more determined to teach that big brown bus a lesson in equine etiquette. Believe me, loading that tack was a formidable one-armed task. Mission accomplished, I gingerly, as not to pressure any point on that virgin uncured cast, led the brown beast to the front of the corral, through the gate, and onto a newly poured and similarly virgin asphalt driveway. Now, the more I considered mounting Hijack, the more exasperated I became with the horse. He was the sole culprit, today's villain, and needed to learn respect without delay. Well, there was no time like the present. Cast or no cast, Hijack was about to face the music.

However, before he could face the music, I had to face his imposing left side, which became a more daunting task than earlier imagined. Teetering on one foot in a struggle to insert the other in that high left stirrup was a challenge with my left arm immobilized. There was no other way but to use my right hand to grip the saddle horn. (Can you keep up with this, horse person?) An awkward beginning rapidly escalated to an even more inelegant ascent as, with one Herculean thrust, I propelled and pulled myself heavenward and toward the summit of the patiently waiting brown beast below. The catapult was well underway with the summit in sight when Hijack inexplicably stopped his patient wait by taking but one baby-step forward.

Well, size of the step aside, his unsolicited action changed the course of my airborne trajectory aft. So, there I was, approaching the zenith of a now perilously out-of-control launch, the unintended second of a very long day, and one where I had no time to find a suitable LZ (landing zone). Fortunately, within the brief but gravity-filled second that followed, I pinpointed a random but less-than-ideal site rushing up to greet me from beneath the beast's big brown belly. Splat!

As a heap sprawled beneath Hijack's looming frame on my now-violated virgin driveway, I noticed the big fella peering around the outside of his left front leg, intently studying the sudden source of chaos. In character, he became detached and resumed his earlier stance, staring directly ahead with monumental disinterest. Completing my second mini-neurological exam of the day, I was instantly grateful that my long arm cast had broken a potentially nastier impact by exploding into a plaster puzzle with innumerable pieces now hanging down like snot from the nose of a two-year-old with a bad head cold. Then I noticed my left fifth finger, throbbing in rhythm with an elevated heartbeat, had distanced itself by forty-five degrees from its neighbor.

Slowly extricating my battered self from beneath the horse's underparts, he continued to remain nonplussed about the whole sordid event. Ruminating, I growled, "But for that one step forward—one unprovoked, unsolicited, and unnecessary step." (Are you getting this full-blown picture of my ever-mounting paranoia, projection, and pity-partying caused by the big brown backyard brute?)

The horse seemed content, almost giddy if horses get giddy, when ushered back to the barn to have his tack removed while given another shot at the feed room. Ignoring my cast's condition, I stumbled back to the hospital for (1) a strident lecture on cast care delivered by the technician and (2) a reapplied long arm cast, now with an enclosed finger splint for my newly fractured pinky.

A full six weeks later, but not a day before, Hijack and cast-free-me again tackled that big hill, chased the coyotes with reckless abandon, but never so much as took one step toward that fateful precipice.

The Happy Departure of Hijack

The time eventually arrived when, as kids do, our girls grew older and lost interest in the horses, who simply loafed around, drew their entitlements, and continued to create stuff for me to repair. One fine day (you can take that as you choose), friends came by and bought Hijack as a barrel racer for their pre-teen daughter. Well, by then, the big brown boy was more than ready to find his niche in life by spending the next fun-filled years running like the wind, chasing barrels instead of coyotes, winning scads of awards, and making his new best friend proud. Duchess also settled into a pleasant setting, and with her departure, our "backyard horse" owner days ended.

Both new sets of owners were well pleased with their horses and raved about their behaviors. We all knew without saying they were yet uninitiated, frankly deceived, openly lying, or trying their best to be civil and make the best of a borderline situation. Our family members now considered themselves full-fledged decorated backyard horse veterans and bore the scars to prove it. We could now speak candidly but with authority about the horse as a paradox, an animal of pleasure and an animal of pain. By the time the dust had settled and keeping up the corral had become a menial chore, the label backyard horse engendered less of an emotionally mixed message. That's the mental quicksand that got me into trouble in the first place, wasn't it? Although the barn, stalls, and feed room stood eerily empty (except for a scattering of hay bales languishing in the latter as mere echoes of a former time), to be safe, came the thought, we needed to empty that feed room of its hay bales and their echoes, mind you, if only to avoid temptation and be delivered from evil (should that big brown bomber boy ever return).

Postscript

Have you ever considered why so many cowboys are the way they are—big, slow, good-natured, and gentle as a Momma's smile? "Howdy, ma'am," they sputter self-consciously, "Niceta meetcha, ma'am." Why are they all so Gary Cooper humble as apple pie, anyway? Know what, were you describing a horse, you would describe him broken. So, you would buy him and give him to your daughter. (Not the cowboy, friend, the horse.) Here is something you may never have considered: How do those cowboys become so mellow? Here is my take. Have you ever been to a rodeo and watched those big guys trying to load their steeds into trailers after the last event? Why, sometimes it is harder than gettin' Momma to a candlelight dinner after the fifth kid. Whinnying, pawing the dirt, planting their hoofs, tossing their heads, and snorting, those beasts are enjoying being ornery. Meanwhile, the cowboys are just mealy mouthing and cajoling and trying to calm the big, spoiled babies down. When you see this, Hopalong, the friendship with Flicka is over. Who's broken? Well, the big, brawny, six-foot-four, 250-pound two-legged pussycats, that's who.

Would you like to know something else? When Hijack got through with me, I was putty in his hands. We had no more disagreements because he had me well-trained, disciplined, and, admittedly, broken. It was not going to take me another long arm cast with a finger splint to accept our mutually shared preferences; the foremost for me was to never again slip the surly bonds of earth while climbing K2 with a "rookie" horse. In my mind, the solution to that conundrum was to stay ahead of that flying fortress, keeping him happy chasing coyotes on the flatlands where you could see forever. Long before my enlightening, Hijack had set that mandate permanently in stone for himself. No way was he going to wait another six weeks between sprints up that big hill to harass Wily Coyote because the "rookie" aboard had all the athleticism of a box turtle. When Hijack went his way, I was believin' him fairly well-satisfied with having me broken. After being mentored by that big brown bus, I would admit to being a tad slower, better-natured, and gentler. All I lacked on his departure was the six-feet-four-inches and two-hundred-fifty pounds needed to become a real cowboy. Truth be told, though, them latter pounds began 'roundin' the bend (if you catch my drift) a whole lot sooner than I ever wished.

"Where," you may ask, "is the Kiss from Heaven in this tale?" Good grief, Roy, everybody still had a pulse!

QUESTION: Where is the Kiss from Heaven from this God Story?

ANSWER: A few years ago, I asked the Lord to allow Emily and me to live through another time of revival, (2) renew in us His ministry to the brokenhearted, (3) complete transcribing the sweet stories we walked together during the last decades, and (4) find a small country farm to care for with a few furry and feathery friends where little Peachy our poochie could finish life running free. Well, here we are on Jerry and Sandra Murphy's Moriah Ranch in Southeast Missouri in revival, surrounded by folks restoring their lives in Jimi and Ladonna Waggoner's Crossroads ministry, putting the finishing touches on His God Stories, and rising mornings to feed every winged critter from hungry cardinals to titmice, roosters Buck and Buck-Buck, Momma Kitty, and a batch of yet unnamed little ones under the house. Then it's on to greet Peachy's three Great Pyrenees buddies here to collect a morning's cookie or two before we are off to the barn to dole sweet feed to grateful Skipper the horse and Pony the pony. It's so beautiful how our God of the second chance has carved out a tender home in our hearts for those elderly equines, filling the void left by those tumultuous years with Hijack and Duchess so long ago. It may have taken a few decades, but if the Kiss from Heaven from that 1970s story didn't satisfy you, maybe, like Emily and me, you can find the goodness of God in the land of the living (Ps. 27:13) and a Kiss from Heaven on steroids in the blessed multi-kissed God Story we are living today.

4

The Hound of Heaven (1974)

Maybe we should wear our Nikes through the hills and dales of this story. We cover a lot of ground. Some of it is smooth, and some may make you stumble. Remember, the only thing in life that is constant aside from God's love is change. And change? It will always bring—well, more change. It was post–World War II and the last half of the 1940s. America was a Christian nation so proud we had set the world free of militarism that by the 1950s, we were, ironically, competing to be the leading militarist in that same world. If you were born in America, at least in my neck-of-the-woods (newly suburbanizing Upstate New York), you were automatically assumed a Christian because you were an American. Asking a Christian if he were a Christian, the answer would more likely be, "I'm an American, aren't I?" Americans kept Jesus's moral teachings because the laws of the land reflected His moral teachings. Nobody polled the Jews about this narrow opinion because none of us knew a Jew or, even if they did, knew a Jew who would admit to being enough of a Jew to be polled. Appears it was not only Germany that had a bias against Jews before my generation even knew what a bias was or any of us had met a Jew. That was until Wally B., who drove a new Lincoln while in high school. Knowing Wally made any recognizable bias positive because Wally was more Christian than most Christians I knew. So, right off the bat, I was a fan of the Jews, although it took twenty years to include Bill and Bob, two Jewish friends as ushers in our wedding, to document that.

Nobody among us knew about this discrimination stuff because that stuff was in the Deep South, and few of us had ever been out of Onondaga County. Had there been a poll taken about that bias stuff, the Negros of yesterday (African Americans of today) who lived in the gullet of the city of Syracuse or the Indians (Native Americans of late) who lived on the Onondaga Reservation south of Nedrow would, for who knows why, have been left out of this "unbiased" polling process. Nobody connected the dots regarding the separated (if not segregated) Polish (aka Polacks), Irish (aka Micks), and Italian (aka Wops) communities in Syracuse, which, had we all known better and been proactive, might have been celebrated as centers of ethical diversity to help keep the lingering animosity between those differing cultures in check. Syracuse's eventual cultural assimilation decades later may have been marked when the city replaced the green light, for generations commanding the top of the traffic signal midway up Tipperary Hill, with a traditional red one (which no self-respecting Irish politician who wished to remain in power ever suggested), and for the first time in history no longer led to the red light's swift demise by a well-placed rock the following night. Incidentally, I am not sure there was a Mexican or Puerto Rican anywhere in Upstate New York, and the name Hispanic had to wait decades to be part of any conversation. And Muslims? Who were they? No one knew enough to ask. Nobody among white Caucasian kids thought a thing about that stuff. For heaven's sake, we were Anglos, crackers, honkies, whiteys, gringos, and white trash even before we knew that was who we were. Could you run fast like (now departed and deeply missed) Bert Hills or shoot a three-pointer (before there was such a thing) like Keith

Brignall? That was all that mattered until girls who had long been a bother suddenly became a matter when Katie McNeil caught my eye while changing seventh-grade classes on as fine an October morning as possible in the year of our Lord, 1952. And church stuff? Well, while many adults went to church, most kids avoided Sunday school unless they had a mother like my mother, who always saw the handwriting on my wall even before there was a wall.

Blue laws following World War II locked down the world tighter than a tic on Sundays to honor the Lord's moral teachings, which, without question, helped fill the churches with those who now had nowhere to go but the churches. Parked cars lined the streets as far as the eye could see (well, at least around Christmas when all little kids, if they prayed, prayed that holy day would fall outside a Sunday). There was no Jewish temple in our village, so Hanukkah slipped by unnoticed. Anyway, while some of us knew about Passover, few could understand how a Jewish lamb could be the Savior of the world.

Sunday school was a drag except for Potty Mouth Woodworth (no blood relative), a kid with such a warped tongue that I told my mother we needed to protect our good name by foregoing Sunday school classes for a while. It is only Christian to admit that Potty Mouth and I remained good buds during the week until that terror-laden night when he used that mouth on all six-feet-ten inches of George Mikan, the Minneapolis (now Los Angeles) Lakers' 245-pound center, following a loss by the Syracuse Nationals (now Philadelphia 76ers) at the war memorial in town. With great regret, I had to add those Nationals games to my list of Sunday school absences, this time not fearing so much for our family's dear name as for my own dear life. Do you understand how threatening a separation of two feet from an irritated six-feet-ten inches of gigantic growling George Mikan can be to a kid slower than a box turtle and yet to conquer four-feet-eight?

Generic Christianity Until...

Genesee Street, aka Route 5, the busiest thoroughfare through our village and the entire Upstate New York, offered three Protestant denominations, all squeezed into one block, along with the Catholics who were a stone's throw up that same main drag. Many, it seemed, had a religious preference; I am a Baptist or Episcopalian, Lutheran, Methodist, Presbyterian, Catholic, or some oil and water mixture of the above was only little more than semi-normative in social exchanges. There wasn't a Protestant among our population of adolescent boys that knew an iota of difference between those denominations. No reason to doubt that. We did, however, understand that the Catholic kids among our Fayetteville Purple Eagles student body had unspoken favor with the school's principal, who excused those kids, one and all, on Wednesday afternoons to do religious stuff with their priest. Meanwhile, that same Catholic principal (who was truly a fine man) would occasionally make a silent wager with himself as grammar school boys duked it out on the playground during recess. With all that, I was a tad confused but fine. That we had to eat breaded fish every Friday lunch for twelve consecutive years, I was not.

No one knew an atheist or an agnostic; the latter was an unfamiliar term that would have needed the use of a dictionary had it come up, which it never did. Besides, both of those beliefs were anti-American, and everyone I knew was not only an American but a patriot who bled red, white, and blue. The only exception was my close friend's older brother, Gordy, who lived in the attic and had a Russian Red Army star pinned to his wall, an emblem that caused me more undue patriotic heartburn than any adolescent kid should have had to endure. Look, a heartbeat ago, we had agonized through and triumphed in the hottest world war of all time and were already in an unwanted cold one with those commies who, it appeared, had already brazenly invaded my friend's attic. Who needed that?

Notice all this took place as a prelim to those rabid evangelicals who invaded our whereabouts during the 1950s led by the late Pat Robertson, who, with a smile, later confessed (and I paraphrase): "We evangelicals invaded the Northeast in the 1950s and were summarily repulsed." It was the beginning of a long-term assault where Bible churches filled with those religious zealots (and their multiple unauthorized non-King James versions of the Holy Bible) eventually arrived to stay in the 1970s, contemporaneous with the Far West's Jesus Movement that never formally made it to Onondaga County. Then, within years but without warning, the door opened (well, was forced open) by the Charismatic Renewal (for which those Catholics must take most blame) and the ensuing craziness that threatened to take our traditional church world captive. For a brief interval, it may have been (had the entire public been polled this time around) a toss-up as to who was considered America's most imminent threat; was it those holy rollers or them commies?

A Witness

By the early 1970s, our family of six was serving a second stint with the military in North San Diego County. Ambushed by a pack of rabid Presbyterians in Pensacola, Florida, my wife accepted Jesus as Savior. Now, "saved" was not a term embraced by the mongrel Northern Baptist-Presbyterians who tutored me as a Christian kid in Central New York State, so I will not use it here. It is also hard to use the adjective rabid to modify the name Presbyterian; doesn't it seem more like an oxymoron? Look, we are talking Presbyterians here, not tongue-talkin' holy rollin' Pentecostals. Now, can you see for good reason, as an American kid who believed in the God of our fathers from his childhood, why he stayed on the fringe of those religious goings-on for years while striving and driving down our country's American-Christian middle-class pipeline toward military and then medical service to humanity? There had always been a not-so-sweet spot in that boy's own personal history where idealism battled ideology. Formal religion to him, it seemed, fit neither.

When my wife became a serious believer, in my mind and from what little I knew as a lifelong (well, at least since my June 13, 1948, ritual dedication) Northern Baptist-Presbyterian mongrel, she was doing a dandy job of it. In the past year, our home had become peaceful (if there could be peace in a home with four kids under the age of ten and waiting upon a fifth), where there was a modicum of respect being given to its paternal figurehead. The covert bitterness in my heart as a shunned Vietnam veteran, erstwhile husband, and sometime eldest child (I had been "gone" for a vast amount of ten years in either military service or medical training) had subsided, and my attitude of attitudes softened. In no way am I assessing blame (which would only be self-inflicted), but confessing that my wife's new way of living had influenced my new way of becoming somewhat more human. Well, I hope you know what I mean.

She faithfully attended a local church on Sundays with the children, leaving me home on Sunday mornings to have down time to ponder life and, inevitably, chew on this religious change in our nuclear family. (Here I was taking "cave time" on Sundays well before "cave time" had legitimately earned the handle "cave time" among the American male species.) As much as I enjoyed home life with our wonderful kids, after hours of reflection in my cave (by now constructed not as a metaphor but by strategically arranged hay bales in the barn's feed room), I concluded that while it might be good for the family, I did not need her kind of religion. Having always believed in God and a need to live a good life, church attendance had still been a dreary episode in my early days when intermittent forays into the children's choir, encouraged by my tone-deaf mother, had drawn only "shh, shhh, shhhh's" from the choir director, who somehow did not share Mom's opinion about this youngster's bright future in music.

Kisses from Heaven, Book Three

A Second Witness

Brother Mac Wright was pastor of the Pomerado Christian Church on the bluff outside Rancho Bernardo, California. That my wife was fond of him was no secret; that she had made it known to Pastor (1) our home was his home, and (2) he was welcome anytime was not made known to me, however. This one-sided agreement was also known to the family's inner circle. Fortunately for me (as the single family member outside the circle), one human member inside its circumference was a whistleblower and blew her whistle, covertly keeping me advised. This "mi casa es su casa" philosophy felt a whole lot like mounting that big brown Hijack horse again (you recall, the one who dispatched me into a fractured wrist and pinky), unsure of the beast from the beginning and legitimately concerned about riding him thereafter.

Now, one of the character traits she admired about Brother Mac was he lived his faith, looking to help people in need, visiting the sick, caring for the widows, and constantly talking about Jesus. He was a witness to all he met. You could not be around the man without hearing about Jesus this and Jesus that. People like the likable Brother Mac were scary, if not altogether weird. And did I mention uncomfortable?

For a while, everything remained under a modicum of control until the pastor, using his get-in-free card, randomly dropped in unannounced weekday evenings and Saturday mornings while I was working around our little ranchette. This birthed a dilemma: Brother Mac was hunting me, mercilessly tracking me down like those rabid Florida Presbyterians had my wife. He had trapped me once early on, and once, my friend, was enough. A plan was essential—a Marine-inspired way of escape and evasion for such times as this. Way too visible outside the house, I devised a scheme . . . you know, like the devil does.

When Brother Mac arrived, he routinely went inside to greet my wife before returning to the yard. That would give me the tactical advantage needed. As Mac entered the home, I would hoof it lickety-split to the barn. Then, when he or my wife came searching, I would be hidden away, safely sequestered deep in my cave, hollowed out among those aging hay bales in the feed room. Believe me, each episode of successful escape and evasion left me subtly proud as a Marine, deeply relieved as an undiscovered backslider, equally ashamed as a coward-in-hiding, and incessantly sneezing as a victim of allergic rhinitis for the rest of the day.

A Third Witness

A grateful man was I, but a marked one. "Predestined," the Bible would say, even "chosen." The hound of Heaven was on my trail, and unknown to this man, his goose was already cooking in the King's kitchen. All those hours strategizing, hiding away in the feed room, and suffering from allergies within those bales were to do no lasting good. What was on its way, however, would.

Okay, let us cut to the chase: A book given to me seemed innocent enough: *Do Yourself a Favor, Love Your Wife*** (which, to no surprise, is still in print). Now, years later, I remember few of that little tome's specifics but recall it being a vehicle that helped change my life. It supplied epiphany. Pure revelation. Mind renewal. Truth.

Truth, I discovered, is an absolute, not an assumption, opinion, logic, common sense, book learning . . . you get it. Truth is a person. Jesus said that He was the way, the truth, and the life (John 14:6). Who He is and what He does is the tangible expression of absolute, not relative, truth. Only an encounter with Holy Spirit, in person or print, can supply absolute truth and that only when we are seekers, open-minded and willing to receive. It is up to Him. He will gladly renew our minds by transforming our ways of thinking with His truth (Rom. 12:2).

The crux? He does it by meeting us where we are (the Holy Bible calls that a "paga"), even when we may not feel His presence, sometimes despite our contrariness, but any time He sees we are primed, ready, and willing. Oh yes, the Word of God is the Spirit of Jesus in print and the standard to which any truth must conform. For Christians, the Bible is their ultimate "fact checker."

Unconsciously, I needed convincing, so God interpreted the book *Do Yourself a Favor, Love Your Wife* in accordance and alignment with His own book, the Holy Bible, further expounded upon it by His Spirit with a rhema word, and brought me the mind renewal (Rom. 12:2) needed. Does that seem weird? Well, yes, it can. Unexpected supernatural encounters often do, mostly because they are what they are, encounters with God often hidden in the ordinary. Sometimes, people simply know in their "knowers."

While reading that book, there were no lights, bells, or whistles. There were no visions, voices, or grand feelings. It was simply a "once I was blind, but now I see" (John 9:25) kind of epiphany. God made sense as He never had. It was what many Christians call an "aha" moment. The veil lifted, and I knew. Leaving the room where I was reading, I entered the kitchen to speak with my wife at the sink: "Your God is now my God." Then, on the following Sunday, I accompanied my family to Brother Mac's church.

A Culmination of Christian Witness

That Sunday, the Pomerado Christian Church was busy with people of all ages, and I was the rookie in the ballpark. Was that culture shock or what? All the folks were talking with or hugging each other as we arrived. Even guys were hugging guys; I shivered. "Oh no, who is this guy coming toward us? Will he try to hug me?" Without hesitating but accompanied by my deep sigh of relief, the man ushered us to the front row. Oh, no, not the front row. A long string of people came by to introduce themselves and welcome the new guy. It was a warm environment, but I was a fish out of water. Nor did I like this front row; I felt conspicuous, scrutinized, vulnerable, and hedged in by all these well-wishers. Strongly wanting to hide in the "way back" of the church quickly gave way to longing for my "cave." Too late, mate. Sigh.

Scrunched down in my pew, I listened intently to the conversations behind me, proclaiming my presence that I was finally there. This intensified my self-consciousness and added discomfort. What was next? Would the pastor make me come forward? Would I have to say something or perform a Northern Baptist-Presbyterian-like ritual? Might I have to confess my sins before the congregation? Oh, how I wished to become invisible. I felt so out of place, isolated among all these strangers, numb inside, and anxious at the same time. This was not what I expected nor why I signed up. Want the truth? I wanted to go home.

Ambushed by Love

Brother Mac came in smiling while welcoming everyone before moving from the pulpit to the piano, where he played, sang, and led the people in worship. Something began to well up in me, an emotion over which I had no control. For my entire life, I had felt alone, unwanted, disconnected, isolated, and out of place for the unfixable person I believed myself to be. I was secretly a lost child who felt he had nowhere to go and nobody to turn to. I spent much of my life among those who loved me, often experiencing a sense of rejection and often despair. It had made me quietly distant, touchy, and angry with life without knowing why.

Suddenly, in a deeply emotional moment (not normative for this Marine Vietnam combat veteran) while seated with my family in the front row before the entire church, I broke down, began to weep and then uncontrollably sob through and past the end of the service while soaking the carpet below with my tears.

What happened in the pulpit that day will always remain a mystery. What happened in that pew never was. Somewhere in that spiritual catharsis, the pain lifted, and I entered a different life, maybe a different paradigm or dimension. Released and set free from the burden of who I was and the world wherein I had lived, tears of grief became tears of joy (Ps. 16:11). For the first time in my life, I felt safe, wanted, welcome, and unconditionally loved (John 3:16). Unaware that I was cocooned in the loving presence of Holy Spirit and His baptism, I finally opened my eyes as the tears subsided. Oh my, the atmosphere was lighter, brighter, and the colors streaming through the church windows more intense.

Above all things, I knew I was a brand-new person. The catharsis over, I stood, looking at a stranger but pews away while suddenly feeling a connection and love for him (1 John 4:16). Holy smokes, I mused, what was that? Holy Spirit had surprised me, had He not? The hound of Heaven had mercilessly tracked me down, exactly as He had my wife in Pensacola. That Sunday, He saved (I could use that word now) my soul and gave me my first official Kiss from Heaven as a born-again Christian without having to speak a word, lift a finger, or have the slightest idea what that new label meant. How was I to know this was merely the beginning?

Postscript

Okay, I was not a biblical scholar, but hadn't I lived through Apostle Paul's epiphany of "wretched man that I am, who will set me free from the body of this death" (Rom. 7:24)? Taught later from the pulpit, that earlier Bible translators often chose the word "grace" to summarize the entire first part of Romans 7:25, "Thanks be to God through Jesus Christ our Lord," as the definitive answer to Paul's question, "Who will set me free?"

"Thanks be to God through Jesus Christ our Lord" (Rom. 7:25): That is a true definition of God's grace if you ponder that shard of Scripture for but a moment. Seeing grace (God's freely giving us the favor that we cannot earn, merit, or deserve but need) must be understood as the only bridge between Rom. 7:24 that accounts for the dramatic change leading to Rom. 8:1, "There is now no condemnation for those in Christ Jesus," confirming John 15:5b, "Without me you can do nothing," to keep us from boasting (Eph. 2:8), and lets us walk freely in the Spirit (Rom. 8:2).

Why is the above important? Well, it shows us how to please the Father and give Him the glory He deserves. Here is the bottom line: Whatever we do will amount to nothing in Heaven (even though we may be a hero of the faith on earth) if we fail to allow Holy Spirit (God's greatest grace gift to all Christians) to bridge the gap (i.e., darkness to light, evil to good, flesh to Spirit) and then be credited for those results. The Holy Spirit of grace sent by Jesus after the cross, resurrection, and ascension is the only bridge for Christians to transform what, by our human effort, God rejects as nothing in Heaven to what will bring Him glory due His name on Earth.

Waiting on the Lord for the privilege to walk in His yoke includes and requires faith, patience, praying, listening, hearing, and obeying the Lord instantly, joyfully, and completely when He calls. When He is ready to work, more can happen during five minutes yoked in His presence than a lifetime of effort spent in the name of God but without Him as our indwelling initiator, prime mover, and glory reaper.

For the better part of thirty-four years, I paid a high price striving and driving on my own with limited success while seeking that morning's Kiss from Heaven given me with no personal effort but freely by the Spirit of grace somewhere during Brother Mac's twenty-minute sermon, not one word of which was heard. So, there I was, a wretched sinner, struggling in a dying body with a dead spirit suddenly born again of the Spirit, a forgiven saint resting alive in Christ Jesus, darkness to light, evil to good, and flesh to Spirit. And wasn't I merely along for the ride across that great divide with the Spirit of grace as my Uber? Exactly why Father gave His Son. Wouldn't you agree?

QUESTION: Where is the Kiss from Heaven from this God Story?

ANSWER: Convinced enough by that *Do Yourself a Favor and Love Your Wife* book to go to church, I also chose to open myself to Jesus as Lord. That is never enough. Had Holy Spirit not ruined me during that Sunday morning's service, I'd have left the building to not return. Being born again is not simply by conviction, decision, choice, or commitment alone but by a miracle resurrection of our dead human Adamic spirit resurrected by the same Spirit that raised Jesus from the dead. Then, one with Him and eternally alive, we may intimately know Him, the power of His resurrection, the fellowship of His sufferings, and be conformed to His death (Phil. 3:10–12). Isn't that the progressive human experience meant every Christian. We cannot reason, white-knuckle, or manipulate ourselves into the kingdom of God. The King and His kingdom come with the born-again experience when old things pass away, and all things become new (2 Cor. 5:17).

Whoa, wasn't that way too much a theological tsunami of thought for me!

"So, Lord, what really happened in that church pew?"

"Well, I saved you, son."

"Saved me from what, Jesus?"

"The wrath of God."

"Oh, that's a plus. Well, then saved to what?"

"Eternal life, to intimately know Abba, your Daddy, and Me, your Savior" (John 17:3).

"Well, Jesus, why didn't you simply say so?"

"I had been saying so for thirty-four years, little brother. A wonderful homecoming, wasn't it?"

Wolf Stories (1979-1997)

Wolves have always fascinated me. All that means is curiosity enough to read wolf-related magazine articles, seek wolf farms, and enjoy sightings in the deep woods but stop short of becoming a compulsive scientific investigator, learned sage, or a politically correct ambassador for these noble creatures. Although having known caretakers for wolfdogs, I have never owned one. Truthfully, nobody ever "owns" a wolf; you coexist with them and mostly on their terms.

Making eye contact with the penetrating gaze of a wolf confirms who is boss in a heartbeat. Hybrids (wolfdogs) can be more agreeable and illustrate how leavening Canis lupus with a little Fido can go a long way to improve relationships between humans and the big bad wolf.

My favorite wolf story, one showing the wolf's intelligence and independent character, comes from a *Reader's Digest* condensed book (undiscoverable to date) published decades ago. Searching for the story for years without success, so please do not hold me to the finer points of this true tale but give grace to fill in the few blanks that time has erased.

A family homesteaded deep in the Alaskan wilderness adopted (more accurately, was adopted by) a gray timber wolf. Canis lupus instantly became a part of the family, was gentle with the children, and turned out to be the father's constant companion as he worked about the spread. One day, the home's only water heater gave up the ghost and, after weeks of waiting for a replacement, the dad, with comrade wolf dozing comfortably in the passenger's seat of the family's old model pickup, left for town to retrieve the new heater. Midway up a steep slope on the way back home, the water heater first slid across the truck's bed and past the open tailgate. Then, careening madly down the recently surmounted precipitous grade, the now not-so-new appliance bounded from bump to stump to end a lump and mere shadow of its former self at the bottom of the hill.

Enraged for not closing the tailgate, the man uncharacteristically threw a full-blown temper tantrum in the driver's seat of the pickup truck. During its stormy course, he caught sight of the wolf sitting bolt upright in the passenger's seat, glaring at him with unmitigated disdain and frank unbelief. As their eyes met, the wolf, repulsed by this sudden uncontrolled outburst, leapt from the open passenger window and rocketed toward the house.

The father confessed that for the next few days, the animal simply avoided him at every turn. Finally, the man realized he had deeply offended the wolf with his lack of emotional control, had lost his respect, and was struggling with whether to let the man continue as the alpha in their relationship. Difficult as it was, the father went to the wolf, humbly prostrated himself before the animal, and apologized. The merciful wolf (how about that for a contradiction?) seemed satisfied and quickly reestablished fellowship with Dad. So illustrates the wolf's pride, intelligence, and requirements for self-control and mutual respect in a relationship. And we, friends, think our marriage relationships can get sticky? How about a crow dinner in front of a wolf?

Waldo the Wolf

Emily, Daisy dog, and I spent the summer of 1997 touring Alaska in our elderly 1977 Class C motor home. Looking back, enduring the

Alcan Highway in a twenty-year-old vehicle dormant in an Oregon wood lot for the previous ten years required not only healthy denial and considerable pluck but a truckload of foolhardiness too. Still, that mighty Dodge 440 took on all comers and, aside from requiring me to roll under her chassis with a hammer to convince the starter's brushes to unseat after most gas stops and frequent pullovers at altitude to adjust a cranky distributor to keep her running smoothly, we cruised merrily through the summer without incident. Someone warned us, "Don't expect to see numerous wild animals as was common along the way in years past. It's simply not the way it used to be." Eighteen grizzlies, even more moose, countless caribou, mountain goats, big horned sheep, deer, elk, eagles, and hawks (I could go on) later, we completed our journey looking for a way to bankroll our 35mm Kodak moments. So much for the Alaskan wildlife naysayers.

Anyway, our single encounter with Canis lupus in the wild was hardly memorable. Heading to Haines, we passed by countless dirt side roads emptying like so many spigots from the thick wilderness onto the main highway. Fifty yards down one inlet, I spied the first gray wolf we had come upon to date. U-turning to pursue the wolf along the permafrost-rutted road, the surrounding woods unexpectedly ended in a broad, barren swath carved from the forest to accommodate high-voltage lines. To our right was our quarry, a large gray standing broadside in the clearing thirty feet from the RV. The wolf, now paralleling our course but moving in the opposing direction, disappeared under cover of the forest before we could catch him on film. Quickly reversing direction and retracing our steps twenty yards, try as we might, we could not spot the animal within the trees. In character, as the legendary gray ghost he was, the wolf had vanished. Disappointed, we snapped a photograph of the timber to have a record of where we had come upon the only timber wolf on our trip to date.

Months later, having returned to Oregon and reviewing a cascade of photographs from our trip, we came upon one glossy that defied explanation. Among all the majestic scenes captured on film was a photograph of a run-of-the-mill stand of timber. At first, we concluded that the camera must have inadvertently discharged, but then came the epiphany: This was the site where we had lost track of that big, beautiful gray entering the tree line. As the first time in the wild, we could discover no trace of the animal in the photograph. Brainstorming, we took a magnifying glass and, under the brightest light available, searched the entire picture for any sign of our elusive wolf. It was like searching for the ever-present but now camouflaged Waldo. Then, eureka, sure enough, in the center of the glossy, standing sideways once again but now deep in the forest between two giant conifers was our long-lost friend. As a bonus, his mate stood behind him, canted forty-five degrees, resting her head on his back, and staring directly at the camera. What was the chance of rescuing that Kodak moment? Decent in God's economy of grace, wouldn't you say?

A Wolf Hostel

Heading north on the west side of the Kenai Peninsula along Cook Inlet eventually takes you to Anchorage and, if you press on, Fairbanks and places even more remote. Somewhere along that route, at a small country market, we came across an advertisement for a wolf farm pinned upon a community billboard. Following its directions, we arrived at a ramshackle building on two acres of property, surrounded by eight feet of weather-beaten corrugated metal fencing. There were no parked cars to convince us the place was open for business. On closer exam, the front door was ajar. As we entered the small store, a tall, affable elderly man with tousled but thinning white hair and matching scraggly beard arrived to greet us. He was available, he said, to show us around his fenced land, which housed forty wolfdogs. The owner explained that not one of his animals was over 6 percent dog; when we finished, all but one, in my eyes, seemed to be anything but pure wolf. The proprietor began by introducing us to his first tenant, a huge gray whose massive head reached my mid-chest (I stand but five-foot-eight-inches.). The wolf dog acted altogether mellow, if not frankly disinterested, during our meeting. We greeted each "wolf" how we might greet any of their dog cousins. The animals would sniff our hands (with a culinary interest in Daisy dog's scent, no doubt) and then patiently let us fondle their dense, wiry hair.

The old man and his wife, our host went on, only adopted abused or abandoned wolf dogs. To "civilize" even the most traumatized and nastiest of his new recruits, the old man used a standard indoctrination: With his wife's approval, he would take each new arrival to their bedroom where, for the first three weeks, the animal slept at the foot of the proprietors' mattress. At the end of those weeks, the old man rarely could not gain the trust of his newest charge. Emphatically, he revealed that love was the answer. Then, he would introduce his new arrival to the rest of the Canis lupus community and to his or her own individual home. He illustrated his success rate by photographs mounted on the walls of the store, which portrayed his wolfdogs "acting" in countless Disney and other wildlife movies. Each animal had a heavy leather collar secured to his "residence" by twelve feet of chain, enough to give the animal ample freedom to move about but not enough to engage his neighbor in a skirmish. Wolves took refuge on top of their dome-like "homes" and seemed very content to kick back and enjoy each other's company from a distance. The only exceptions were a wild, pure black female wolf caged in the center of the enclosure and one lone male hybrid who fiercely contested the old man's right to be the "alpha" male. As the owner approached this wolfdog, the enraged animal charged to the end of his chain with teeth barred, growling fiercely, and with all that was within him, tried to attack his adversary. Instructed to treat this animal like the rest, I first believed the man joking. He was not. With reluctance and not-so-hidden fear, I moved toward the big gray once his "adversary," the proprietor, had slipped out of sight. As had all the others, this enormous wolf dog greeted me with dignity and reserve. That I was no threat to him remained clear; that this wolfdog had not yet reached anywhere near that conclusion with his adversary alpha was as certain. That saddened me, knowing how the man loved that animal and what that wolfdog was missing.

The caged female had two pups sired by an exceptionally large but exquisitely gentle male I had met earlier. The female pup was affectionate and enjoyed being fondled and loved. The male had the wild of his pure black-haired mother and shrunk back, whining as I approached. While seeking his acceptance, another vehicle pulled into the parking lot next to our motor home. Daisy, our seven-year-old border collie-pug-beagle mix, who most misidentified as a Welsh Corgi, immediately barked to guard her territory. Without hesitation, the entire city of wolfdogs began howling with a gleeful intensity. Imagine forty crooning wolves, muzzles lifted toward heaven, harmonizing in unison. What an incredible sight and sound! Astounded, the old man told us to cherish this moment as this bunch rarely howled in the least.

The two-minute melody gradually subsided. Within five more minutes, however, another car pulled into the lot, and, under Daisy's direction and to the old man's delight, the whole musical interlude ignited again.

We made one final trip around the giant kennel and then reluctantly left covered with enough wolf hair to be the Wolfman himself. Daisy went a little berserk when we climbed into the rig. Drawn to the wolves' scent on our clothing and then physically repulsed when smelling it, we could see in her heightened excitement followed by almost palpable fear. Emily and I will never forget that special day. Daisy, we thought, would prefer not to remember it, but unsure why.

Flying Wing on a Wolf

Without question, the most memorable up-close-and-personal encounter with Canis lupus in the wild was my first. It was 11:00 p.m. on New Year's Eve in 1983 when my eldest son and I challenged the logging roads, which crisscrossed the mountains due west of our home on Dorena Reservoir in Western Oregon on three-wheelers. We encountered a dark, overcast, moonless night journeying toward a summit north of the Bohemia Mountains and into a ferocious blizzard. Cresting the mountain and into a six-inch blanket of fresh snow, the large swirling flakes severely restricted our sight of the pristine but unmarked path before us. While surmounting a substantial incline in a gradual right-hand turn, an enormous timber wolf, tufted ears perked, covered in snow, and clothed in his bushy winter coat suddenly appeared as a specter from the darkness to challenge us for control of the road.

Traveling at twenty miles per hour, the interval between our bikes and the wolf closed rapidly. Defiant, the animal seemed ready to confront this intrusion into his solitary world by not giving an inch. While I was more than ready to relent, instead, the wolf turned and easily loped on fifteen feet ahead. No more speed was available from the 200cc Yamaha, and the wolf seemed satisfied with the separation. Then, without warning, he darted over the embankment, taking a short roadway leading, I was aware, to a closed and abandoned gate about twenty-five feet down that hillside. Within seconds, up pops Mr. Wolf to reestablish his earlier path and speed, his shoulder now only six inches from my handlebars. Oh my, here was my New Year's Kiss from Heaven to last a lifetime.

The lights from my bike silhouetted his massive head, tufted ears, and the rough outline of his body lunging effortlessly along beside me. No more than twelve inches from the three-wheeler, the giant wolf's back was even with my shoulders. As a former Naval aviator, I could only think of one thing: "This is Delta X-Ray Three Zero Seven, I'm flying wing on a wolf, over." I so wanted to touch the boy, could easily have done so, but thought better of the idea (a decision instantly elevated to one of the more respectable pieces of headwork of my entire life). After thirty seconds, the wolf punched his passing gear, sped ahead in a flash, crossed before our lights, and disappeared up the steep embankment to our right.

Speaking with the Bureau of Land Management the following week, I found there had been occasional wolf sightings in our area. Catching sight of one-hundred-fifty pounds of adult wolf in the wild is one thing; flying wing on him with a three-wheeler is something far different. Do you think that majestic creature felt my awe, amazement, and gratitude? Maybe my interest in brief companionship was mutually intriguing? Or was he simply indulging me? He could have separated from us anywhere along the line but felt comfortable enough to hang out for a couple of moments. Happily, how blessed I am to tell and relive this wonderful story as a "Kiss from Heaven" at my leisure. You know, I wager that big gray boy had a story to tell too.

Postscript

What has always intrigued me about wolves is their air of detachment, remarkably akin to how a New York debutante views a coming-out party in Newark, an Ivy League alum a guy with a diploma from PS 31, or a gourmet chef with a burger flipper from McDonald's. Canis has a poorly concealed air of intolerance camouflaged by sophistication, intellect, and deadly confidence, all rolled into a rippled one-hundred-fifty pounds of professional meat-eating assassin. That should tell us a little something about any wolf.

Aside from "lone wolves," who generally are not strong enough to earn a place of respect in the pack before they are driven away, and a few pack members, especially the omega wolf, upon whom everyone takes out their bad-hair days, the rest work hard together to hunt, raise their offspring, and train them to be resolute and responsible members of the pack. Like other species (which we will not mention), they also have the bad habit of leaving their elderly and the infirm behind to be recycled in the wild. They are no-nonsense, cerebral, and pragmatic animals, although I have seen them kick back, play happily, and wag their tales like Fido. That is about where the similarities end.

Wolves have taken hits over the "wolves in sheep's clothing" thing, which would imply they somehow need to be deceptive. They are too proud and frankly corporately too strong and disciplined to resort to such tactics, despite the Red Riding Hood fiction. That would be beneath their dignity. Their politically incorrect Achilles' heel would be the caste system of the pack. It seems excessively important to be the top dog (although they would not choose those words) only because being the alpha wolf instantly causes all the females to give up their cell phone numbers. The pack's structure has all the rigidity of the Italian civil service. The omega wolf, a source of irritation to everyone else, finds itself at the bottom of the social food chain, can never brew the coffee properly, run the copy machine without getting a paper jam, and is always on a "break."

A wolf's one glaring social weakness has always been relating to other species whom the pack evaluates only by how long they might last outside the freezer. It is really an attitude problem since in Canis's mind, all species are endangered species. Wolves are not looking for relationships, friendships, or even acquaintances outside the pack. They are looking for food. Just food. So, men, like deer, elk, and any other species, need to understand that just because he looks like a big gray "Rin-Tin-Tin," he is not. He is, instead, beneath that calm, assured exterior, a highly trained, dispassionate serial killer who sees you as a light lunch. If you can convince the wolf that you are alpha material by carrying an automatic magnum (not champagne, Bubba), which is about the only thing he and his cronies respect about man, you might have a chance. If not, you might consider staying in east Chicago, where your odds may be a tad better.

Lighten up, folks. Hyperbolizing, I am, once again. Still, this teaching clarifies why Jesus held a higher-than-normal alert for "wolves in sheep's clothing," does it not (Matt. 7:15)? If only to be reminded of that warning's relevance in these last times, Christian, might be enough to qualify this tale as today's Kiss from Heaven.

QUESTION: Where is the Kiss from Heaven from this God Story?

ANSWER: The owner of the wolf farm became ecstatic hearing the unified response from over 4000 combined pounds of forty mighty wolf dogs to the threat of one obedient twenty-five pounds of poochie. It put a chill down my spine to see a pack of ravenous wolves ready to gang up on one little outsider for merely following her master's orders to guard the car. It also reminded me of a time when an Oregon pastor and hand-picked board of elders decided one devoted local Christian doctor with a gift to heal and deliver the brokenhearted among Pastor's flock became a little too visible, appreciated, and soon judged a false teacher. So, one lovely Sunday morning, as the wolves set to howling, one valiant lone elder left the platform for a second time (following a completed time of prayer ministry by the elders to the entire congregation down front) to minister Jesus' love to our beleaguered brother (left prayerless and alone at the altar in full view of the pastor, the remaining elders, an entire congregation, and a cloud of Heaven's witnesses). No need to elaborate except to say there are wolves who pose as sheep and, regrettably, sheep that act like wolves. Then, praise Jesus for His good shepherds who leave the ninety-nine to rescue the one (Luke 15:3–7). You know, like the never-to-be-forgotten rescue and Kiss from Heaven I received from my courageous brother, elder, and good shepherd, Bruce Andrew.

The Bushel of Corn (1980)

Wednesday evening's service was a simple but refreshing time of worship at the Cottage Grove Faith Center held in the vacated Mount View School, reluctantly forsaken by our local school district reeling from the effects of the worst economic downturn in America's wood products industry in recent memory. The year was 1980 when, in that old, rambling, whitewashed landmark situated just east of town on a country road winding its five-mile way toward pristine Dorena Reservoir, our Pastor Rob would gather his flock and strum a veteran twelve-string guitar as we sang contemporary Maranatha praise songs to the Lord. Though these times always created a slow-paced and devoted sense of worship, recently, that worship had become an uncharacteristically difficult stretch of faith for those salt-of-the-earth Christians present.

A Time of Struggle

While most of our country struggled through the scandalous years of inflation during the Carter administration, Oregon in the early 1980s was suffering in the black hole of a backbreaking recession. Historically, all our state's economic eggs had been in the wood products industry's basket. New businesses, if they had not avoided Oregon altogether, hastily left when they discovered the smothering business tax code and, just as imposing, the radical "philosophical" resistance of certain segments of the population to any new growth in the slightest. Oregon was even then in the embryonic throws of its evolution into a "green" state, years before the rest of the country would have a clue as to what that politically correct word eventually meant.

Finding the previous carte blanche practices of the lumber products industry under increased scrutiny by public and private watchdog agencies, companies like Weyerhaeuser and Georgia Pacific were not only being crippled by a lack of demand for wood products throughout the country (as the housing industry languished) but also found their day-to-day operations beleaguered by the "tree-hugging" tactics of a radical environmental left. Driving six-inch spikes into the giant firs to disable faller's chain saws or roping themselves as sacrificial lambs among their branches to hinder harvesting operations, the activists further hindered both logging operations and the faltering financial well-being of its already severely reduced workforce.

Creating a Culture

Along with other folks, I have often wondered if the relentless westward push in the early years of our nation by fiercely private and intensely proud mountain men did not culminate in the Northwest evolving into a hotbed of rugged individualism. Pioneers and their families, fueled by constant urban pressure at their heels, intermittently settled and then uprooted their way across the country, East to West, only to inevitably meet the vast Pacific Ocean and the unwelcome end of their journeys. The hard-nosed, stiff-necked spiritual climate of the Northwest created by the accumulation of these like-minded, unsettled, and often rebellious souls would, over the next generations, heartily accommodate the eventual influx of immigrating North Carolina and Arkansas loggers, whose tough-minded attitudes and hedonistic lifestyles comfortably fit the molds of their "mountain man" predecessors. Finally, in the latter years of the tumultuous sixties, Oregon had become a magnet to the surviving remnants of an aging, ponytailed, tie-dyed, Birkenstock-shod, free-spirited, me-centered hippie generation. Then, over the following decade, hordes of intensely hostile loners followed—Vietnam veterans who had surged steadily into her endless forests to take up home after that unpopular conflict. The penchant for those latter folks to live along the banks of her desolate rivers or trespass deep within her boundless woodlands revealed the wild at heart, self-gratifying, and anti-authoritarian attitudes that had gradually become "classical" marks of an unstable Great Northwest ethos. Lately, we can add a growing embryonic culture of anarchy and a penchant for protesting many traditional societal restraints, which have caused crime to rise, cities to fall into disrepair, homelessness to grow, and tax-paying populations to wither.

This simplistic explanation helps clarify why the states of Oregon and Washington have ended up as the two least "churched" states in the nation while concurrently developing left-leaning major state universities, blue-tinged politics, and a voting system by referendum that encouraged early activist causes spanning the spectrum from animal rights to assisted suicide, gun regulation, universal medical care, same-sex marriage, transgenderism, and on to its new children of anarchy and entitlement. Years ago, secular humanists and postmodernists saw the Northwest as an opportunity to help each other shape society to their liberal liking, while Christians saw this area of our country as a white harvest field. Little has changed.

Recession

When the state's lumber mills finally closed in the early 1980s under the burden of recession, thousands of workers, often pulling down an hourly wage of double-digit figures per hour and $50,000 yearly, faced sudden impossible financial hurdles, not the least of which were home mortgage payments on notes approaching 19 percent interest.

Within months, enormous numbers of Oregon's front lawns bore "For Sale" signs. Predictably, one by one, Western Oregon cities lost population as unemployed citizens either sold their properties at a loss or simply walked away to greener pastures as their only workable alternative to financial ruin. As a local family doctor, I found my accounts receivable swelling to more than $100,000 (a staggering amount for a general practitioner at the time) due to my collection rate dropping well below 70 percent. So, I settled for firewood, handyman labor, farm animals, eggs, and other alternative payment options from those patients who insisted on meeting their obligations one way or the other. These were the hard-pressed and industrious people to whom our pastor delivered his message that Wednesday night, proud people suffering economic hardship few had ever experienced.

A Gift from the Heart

Pastor was concluding our Wednesday night's service, unavoidably ending my unintentional power nap with last-minute announcements I heard sparingly. One that caught my ear suggested we parishioners, on our way home, take as much of the freshly picked sweet corn as we wished from a bushel basket strategically placed in our line departure on the front porch of the church. The corn was a love offering from the home garden of one unselfish church family trying to ease the economic burdens of others in our congregation. Soon, folks were slowly ambling through the big front door, past that brimming bushel of corn, and quietly bidding each other good evening on their way home. By now, I was surfacing from the comfort of a warm sanctuary, zipping up my jacket, and mentally preparing to plunge into a crisp autumn evening. I so enjoyed Wednesday nights. They were a balm, a wonderfully soothing way to come off a hectic hump day and find tranquility before heading to a home spilling over with the collective activity of our five children. Tonight, however, I had a couple of things to share with the pastor on our way out, so I waited lazily in my pew while he tended to the questions from a lingering handful of folks more needy, I assumed, than myself.

There were but the two of us left as I joined Pastor in turning out the lights to exit the darkened building. The front porch light, intentionally left burning 24/7, highlighted a bushel basket overflowing with sweet corn, tassels still clear and untarnished on this crystal night lit by an ivory-colored harvest moon hanging directly overhead.

Abruptly, Holy Spirit interrupted my ongoing conversation with the pastor with this whisper, "I want you to take that entire bushel of corn home." Instantly startled and then outright resistant, "Lord," I thought, "we have had our share of corn this fall. Besides, taking that entire bushel would be impolite, even rude, considering so many of these folks are indigent and without work."

Holy Spirit countered, "What folks?" as I looked around. Well, there was Pastor who, I had to admit, also held down a steady job.

Obedient but reluctant, I asked, "Pastor, are you going to take any of this corn with you?"

"No," he replied.

"Well," I mumbled, "would you mind if... if... I took the bushel with me," feeling more than a touch embarrassed for seeming needy, greedy, or something less than an others-centered "Christian."

"Help yourself," he was quick to answer. Backtracking, I picked up the corn and, finishing our conversation, placed it into the rear seat of my elderly Suburban as Pastor left the parking lot.

A Lesson Learned

Shivering in harmony with the old Chevy as he warmed himself up, I wondered why the Lord had directed me to take every ear of that bushel. Without my asking, Holy Spirit answered, "A family grew this corn to bless others; how can I return and multiply blessings to them when no one is willing to receive their love gift in the first place?"

(This is as cogent and succinct a paraphrase of what I remember and the gist of the Lord's more exhaustive response.) Point taken; theologically, it made sense. Sowing and reaping is an immutable principle of Heaven; how could those selfless gardeners reap any good thing from their generosity if no one in the congregation would receive it? Didn't I know that; had I not known it forever? The problem in my little nutshell of a world was I realized, with more remorse than expected, that I never practiced it. This daunting revelation was powerful, pierced my heart, left me confused and, as I recall, kind of like being run over by a truck in a good way.

History Matters

Growing up, my nuclear family had considered itself fiercely independent and resolutely self-sufficient. We prided ourselves on diligence, demanding work, always completing the task at hand and, most meaningful of all, doing it on our own with no outside help. Two immutable principles conditioned us from childhood: "If you want something bad enough, you can achieve it," and "You can be anyone you choose to be if you work hard enough." Our parents had struggled through the Great Depression, always providing for themselves and their children. They received no neighborly, family, church, or government help. They did it on their own by the sweat of their brows.

Watching, I had learned my lessons osmotically throughout my youth as my well-intentioned father extended the flat of his palm toward others who offered us help. "No thank you," he would affirm, "we are fine. Thank you, anyway." Then I saw my sister, followed by my brother and, finally, myself, entering the same pattern of behavior. We did not need another soul; we could do it all on our own. We were, it appeared, very private people, fiercely proud and independent. We were, without knowing, the rugged individualists of our own generation (ones, I parenthetically mention, among the few that never moved west; well, at least until then).

When I saw this way of reasoning as my "truth" and a huge part of my belief system, I was shocked—no, more like crushed. What had I done? Who had I become? Everything I cherished about tenaciously pressing through life, ignoring any help offered on the way, and then priding myself on reaching every finish line alone was the antithesis of everything that I had heard tonight from the Lord. That meant that I had spent my entire life going against Heaven, not so much about giving but everything about receiving. While considering I had been unselfish, thoughtful of others' time, and caring for their priorities by being self-reliant, I had denied them the chance to receive multiplied blessings from the Lord each time I refused their gifts or labors of love. But, I shivered, why should I have expected them to receive mine? Knowing that each self-centered event needed repentance and forgiveness, I quickly found that daunting process would not happen in a day.

A Point Well Taken

Driving home, the Lord impressed upon me through my tears that every man and woman leaving the sanctuary that evening, including the pastor and myself, received the same opportunity to bless tonight's gift giver. Except for the Lord taking me by the scruff of the neck, that corn, brimming with all its potential blessings for both the "sower and the eater," would go to waste. All this because everyone's singular focus concerned only what that corn could do for them, the "eater," and not what it meant to the "sower." (Have we considered that every gift we gratefully receive from Holy Spirit blesses Him?) It is simple, isn't it? Receiving becomes the essential selfless response to an act of giving and opens the door to exponential blessings for the giver. Long after that night and its lessons, I continue to struggle with ways to humble myself and freely receive from others in the sowing/reaping economy of God. It has taken years of obedience to that teaching to restrain myself from automatically extending that proud palm but open it toward those who wish to sow God's love gifts into my life.

Looking back, Oregon turned out to be my ideal fit; what better place for a fiercely independent, rugged individualist who privately needed no one to help him out, could do it all on his own, and had mastered the palms out, "No thanks, but thanks anyway," couplet to perfection. Can you see why, to this day, I am always grateful when reminded that were it not for a Kiss from Heaven on one exquisite, moonlit autumn night on the porch of a little church in the old, white-washed Mount View grade school outside Cottage Grove on the road winding its way toward pristine Dorena Reservoir?

Postscript

Ever since I passed my seventieth birthday well over a decade and a half ago, I have been waking up to squeeze each new day like a big juicy Florida orange and then consume it like that "good to the very last drop" cup of Maxwell House. Finishing my journey on this earth with boots strapped on, busy about our Father's business, pleasing Jesus, and following hard after Holy Spirit now gives special meaning to life. So, extending and receiving forgiveness, mending broken hearts, sharing needed words, building bridges, spending time with friends and family, blessing the church, and seeing the afflicted and needy set free are but part of the bushels of corn languishing as gifts on my overcrowded but well-lit front porch. How has that happened? Well, on more days than I wish, while watching the tassels of that sacrificial maize dry out before my eyes, go wanting, and then to waste, I have come to deeply understand how we steal others' blessings when we refuse to accept each other's gifts.

People around us immersed in striving and driving, busyness, distraction, performance, a need for independence and self-sufficiency, sin, competition, materialism, religion, dissatisfaction, worry, unresolved bitterness, or blind pride (name more, if you choose) have little time or inclination to receive another's sacrificial gifts with humility or gratitude. When others do not make themselves good ground to seed another's blessings, where are we to take all those idle and unwanted bushels stacked up on our metaphorical front porches before they spoil? Well, if our preoccupied Christian friends and families are unwilling to receive, how about heading to the homeless shelters in our cities, orphanages in Romania, AIDS babies in Uganda, persecuted Christians in the Middle East, widows of India, children living in the dumps of Matamoros or in refugee camps the world over?

"To the extent that you did it to one of these brothers of Mine, even the least of them," Jesus once said, "you did it to Me" (Matt. 25:40). Sounds like there might be a bunch of return blessings (Kisses from Heaven) in those ministries outside our often-sleepy organized American Church, doesn't it?

If it gives you any consolation, here is something to ponder: If you are feeling sad about ending up with an empty cornfield, free bushels brimming with silver-tasseled ears ignored on your crowded front porch, and few blessings to show for your sacrificial effort and hard work, consider how our Lord grieves over an empty cross, a world full of lost souls extending their proud palms toward His free gift of eternal life, and way fewer salvations than He deserves for His sacrificed body and shed blood.

Puts things in perspective, doesn't it, Christian?

QUESTION: Where is the Kiss from Heaven from this God Story?

ANSWER: The Lord is often subtle in bringing His truth about love to our lives. How a bunch of Christians chose not to partake of a free bushel of freshly picked sweet corn offered to the congregation was a creative way to bring me up short on that crispy autumn evening. Knowing it is selfish not to give was always a given. That it is equally self-centered not to receive leads us to understand how the Lord looks at the whole sowing and reaping process. Most of us believe that when you give a true love gift, all you wish in return is love. So what makes us so ethnocentric to intentionally deny others' ways to express love so they might also receive a blessing?

One reason: We feel ourselves unlovable, so love gifts from others remind us of that powerful lie, which commonly arises from a misinterpretation of earlier trauma, causing us (as neglected or abused children or heavily traumatized adults) to identify and feel ourselves unlovable. That conclusion never lines up with God's truth. Jesus dying for us should eliminate that lie and negate its feelings. John 3:16 should relegate it to history. But neither reason rarely does.

That lie (we are unlovable) blocks us from receiving love from God or others while requiring us to manage pain coming from that false belief or its progenitors (i.e., I am undeserving, worthless, flawed, not enough, inadequate, etc.). Refusing others' love gifts (or hiding them out of sight) helps us avoid feeling like unworthy hypocrites. Let us be clear: Were we able to receive those gifts in love and later sacrificially pass them on in God's economy, they would become a blessing for all concerned. But we do not; although the gifts may be eventually passed on to mitigate our feelings of hypocrisy and appreciated by others, the process becomes irrelevant to Heaven as an unrecognized gaslight to the second recipient.

Oh, haven't we dug a deep well today, hopefully deep enough to discover the unique traumatic memory misidentifying us as unlovable? If so, and we release the anger, resentment, bitterness, hatred, rage, vengeance, etc., toward the perpetrators used to shield us from the emotional pain flowing from that memory, then Holy Spirit will act to restore our God-given identity (always lovable). Accomplishing the above opens all doors to uninhibited agape love between both the sower and reaper (giver and receiver), making love gifts take on deeper meaning to both Earth and Heaven. Talk about a revolutionary Kiss from Heaven.

It Takes a Village (1982)

It was a dark and stormy night! Not really, but this brief hackneyed literary springboard aptly sets the metaphorical stage for the ensuing melodrama. If this story were not true, you would dismiss it as the figment of an old man's clouded sensorium, the product of a misguided wannabee comedian, or a tale narrated by a sleep-deprived doctor who does not know the first thing about a patient's privacy. Well, feel proud; you would be right any way you looked at it.

Life's Only Constant Is Change

Back in the late 1970s, there was a groundswell movement in our state of Oregon to take, I cannot express it any more succinctly, medicine out of medicine. Let me explain. Activists linking arms with holistic practitioners, everyone from naturopaths to chiropractors to aroma therapists to kinesiologists, nearly took the state health system hostage. Well, it felt that way. With this revolution, medical consumerism rose like Godzilla taking on Mothra while scaring the Hippocratic pants off every medical doctor over the age of thirty. Anyway, that was my take on the whole sordid event. However, after further soul-searching, critical analysis, and compassionate appraisal of our patients' needs, we Oregon medical doctors acquiesced to this pressure to go with the political flow. (Actually, we were coerced, soundly thumped, and then overrun, but too supercilious to admit it.)

The Birthing Room

In our little hospital's case, that "flow" was in part represented by the "birthing room," an unconventional place devoid of any reminders of proud past medical professionalism to any doctor crossing its threshold to bring life into this cruel world. After decades of delivery rooms with their familiar iron-clad tables, stirrups, anesthesia machines, sterile instruments, and green-garbed mannequins, our new-age medical consumerism thrust us doctors into a room with a bed. That was all, a bed. Okay, also a chair or two . . . and a table. And, later, a fetal monitor. But that was all. We were undone. Now sit back, relax, and let me take you into those Spartan surroundings and to a new episode of "Abbott and Costello Meet in the Birthing Room." (That's right, I am carbon dating again.)

Meet Our Cast

Jillsey (an eastern Oregon cowboy kind of girl) and Gig (a shy retiring lad whose name I am spelling in reverse to preserve his anonymity) were newlyweds pushing one year. They had armed themselves thoroughly with Lamaze classes, intense scientific investigation of the birthing process, and, only then, proudly claimed to have devised a sound, well-thought-out set of birthing room principles. I felt a tad peripheral to the entire process, but since Gig's dad was a friend and the town's mayor, I agreed to stay on the sidelines doing periodic checks, writing vitamin prescriptions, and offering comments like, "You are doing fine," and "See you in a month." After thirty days, when the couple would return for their next visit, it was always with a hearty, "We are still pregnant." Usually, I only checked Jillsey. Consumerism, you can see, had yet to conquer my entire life.

Well, the big day arrived, and I met the kids in the birthing room in the afternoon, as I recall. Well, that is not altogether correct since I met them along with their parents, siblings, next-door neighbors, and a handful of close friends. "Extended family is on the way," Jillsey chirped, her hand held securely by Gig, hovering at arm's length. Smiling, I left the room to find the obstetrics nurse on duty. From what I could see, tonight, we might need all the help we could muster.

Getting Underway

For a fact, Jillsey was doing fine for a "primip" (the abbreviated doctor lingo for primigravida, which is complicated Latin lingo for first pregnancy). Gig was also doing fine; let's include him here because it was, in those budding days of equality, his first pregnancy too. People kept arriving. Then, supper hour came and nearly went before someone suggested pizza. Within minutes, there were burgers, fries, soft drinks, and two enormous pizza pies floating around the room. By now, not only extended family had entered our little birthing commune, but I took curious note, a couple of chamber of commerce people thinking it politically correct (well before that term was coined) to be at the birth of the mayor's first grandchild.

His Honor had been busily placing a video camera on a tripod, strategically (if not boldly) looking true north from the foot of the birthing room's bed. Fine-tuning its innovative location, he retreated to one of the small groups of "lobbyists" to share his gregarious personality with all who were interested. Everyone was having a wonderful time; a little rendition of "Take Me Out to the Birthing Room" would have fit the occasion fine and dandy. Then, all we needed would be popcorn . . . oops, sorry, there it was, right next to the Cracker Jacks, Dr. Pepper, chucks, four-by-fours, and a sterile tray standing at the ready for episiotomy repair. While the entire gathering was busy socializing and enjoying the moment, Gig and Jillsey were understandably more preoccupied with their "philosophy."

A Slow Start to a Long Journey

"Okay, now breathe," Gig would assert, huffing and puffing in synchrony with Jillsey until one of them became lightheaded, approached a faint, or her contractions became discouraged. Placing my hand on Jillsey's belly (palpating her uterus for interested health care types) to check her contractions and Doppler the baby's heartbeat, I was frankly unimpressed. But then, I was merely the doctor groping my way through this new land of consumerism ravaging its way through my once-familiar world of medicine.

"Could we have everyone leave the room, please? Doctor needs to check the patient's progress," trumpeted Ms. Nurse in her command voice. Out they filed only to return, challenging each other through the doorway like Jerry Garcia's faithful Deadheads fighting for the last dozen seats of a Grateful Dead concert. It appeared to me, at least, we could use a little crowd control.

"What if we have a fire with all these people crowded here?" I pled unsuccessfully while looking for a sympathetic ear. "We could all suffocate, burn to death, or be trampled underfoot in the escape." Ms. Nurse smiled. The smell of my cooked goose was in the air long before her patronizing look. It was the way things were to henceforth be . . . folksy! Nurses loved folksy. Consumers loved folksy.

Jillsey, however, could not care less at this point about folksy. She had made little progress and was vociferously complaining about her discomfort. The Gigster, recently swept back into the room with that tide of Deadheads, looked a little concerned but a whole lot lost. In his eyes, I could see this day had rapidly and uncontrollably deteriorated into much more than expected.

A Snail's Pace

Now, you can go crazy if you keep checking your watch during someone's labor. Without saying, the doctor is always checking his watch to monitor the patient's contractions. So, the doctor will always go crazy, not only counting minutes between contractions but thinking of the charts he must dictate, the hospital rounds he has yet to make, and the football game he is missing.

However, and to my delight, the room had once again become festive with conversation and the laughter that follows any delightful repast while Jillsey's contractions were coming more often, happily lasting longer and increasing in intensity. At the next check (tide of people out), her progress was encouraging (tide of people in).

Within brief minutes, Jillsey and Gig's duet sounded like "The Little Engine That Could." Huffing and puffing in unison, although Gig was making no progress, Jillsey was making quite a bit. That fact lifted my spirits, but not so much hers.

"These hurt," Jillsey broadcast, as if genuinely taken by surprise. "Not sure I can do this. I need medicine. Yes, medicine," she then concluded with authority not to be questioned.

"Breathe now," countered Gig, earnestly executing his assignment with the tone of a dutiful Boy Scout escorting a child across a school crossing.

"Give me medicine," rudely interrupted Jillsey, "give me medicine!"

"No medicine in the birthing room," admonished Sgt. Major Nurse with a disapproving look. Medicine in the birthing room, we grew to understand, was like cursing in church; do not even think about it. But then, as I thought about it, we were by no means in church. Thank goodness, we soon agreed.

A Speedbump

"I NEED SOME @#$#^%$*&&^ MEDICINE," bellowed Jillsey, her voice suddenly jumping two octaves in a crescendo approaching one hundred decibels, briefly reminding me of the Oregon Ducks game I was missing at Autzen stadium.

"Breathe, now!" interrupted the well-intentioned but now increasingly irrelevant Gigahubby, empathically on cue but lacking the best of timing. Regrettably, that well-meant morsel of ill-timed relevance became the proverbial straw that broke the poor camel's back.

Oh, my goodness, right before our very eyes, Jillsey, pivoting in her comfy birthing bed like a point guard facing an opponent's frantic attempt at a buzzer-beater, confronted her husband's sudden chauvinistic challenge for her to breathe. Eyes narrowed to the slits of a cobra's, she spat across the four-inch abyss separating her beet-red face from Gig's gray-green one; "GET OUTTA HERE," she hissed, punctuating that command with thunderous run-on seconds of "NOWWWWWWW!"

Intermission

Whoa, Nellie, you could have heard a pin drop. Like imbedded guerrilla night fighters routed from a strategic vantage point, the room's entire cadre, clothed in the embarrassing silence of vicarious reprimand, began to slide toward the safety of the birthing room's exit. Without comment, nuclear family, extended family, close friends, neighbors, acquaintances, and political opportunists swiftly followed Gig's slinking retreat into the arms of that blessed demilitarized hallway.

Looking around, nobody was left but Jillsey, Ms. Nurse and the doctor. "Comfortable and quiet," I mused, "just like the old days . . . minus the stirrups and green-garbed mannequins, of course."

The Home Stretch

We turned toward Jillsey, who was now far less anxious than determined. Suddenly, like the true rodeo queen from eastern Oregon she was, it was time to saddle up and ride this pony. Twenty minutes later, with a whole lot of work and encouragement, we watched her lasso a healthy little cowpoke. Then, with baby in arms and extending forgiveness to all, she welcomed her adoring subjects back into court with no one the worse for wear. People were smiling, soon laughing, crying, hugging, congratulating one another, and reaching for cold pizza. It was wonderful. Reminding myself once again of why we subjected ourselves to such dizzy scenarios (well, not this dizzy), I completed the newborn exam and surveyed the whole wondrous show one last time; everything was in order. Time to go. There were charts to dictate, rounds to make, and the results of a ballgame to catch.

The mayor's video camera, relentless in its pursuit of the naked truth, faithfully captured this entire Kiss from Heaven. Under a twisted sense of duty (well, plus a little love), I watched the whole birthing room "Barnum and Bailey" wannabe again (without charge this time, I might add). Jillsey and Gig, I wager, shared it a zillion times with half the town. And why not? Had it not been a consumer's delight and, beyond all things, real folksy?

Postscript

We might be a little less tongue-in-cheek and more serious for a paragraph or two. Naval aviators (been there, done that) have a well-seasoned axiom: flying military aircraft amounts to hours and hours of sheer boredom interrupted by moments of stark terror. Believe me, obstetrics is little different; like military aviation, delivering newborns requires good headwork (i.e., careful planning, mindfulness, constant monitoring, competent management of each commonplace occurrence, and rapid intervention into any crisis event). Emergencies are scheduled in neither aviation nor obstetrics, but they occasionally occur in the friendly skies of civilian airliners as well as in the folksy confines of a birthing room.

This sweet little Kiss from Heaven paints a lighthearted portrait of two young folks sharing a beautiful, commonplace delivery with their family and friends in the early 1980s. And why not? On a more sobering note, we all understand that, although all guests enjoyed themselves during that gathering, the doctor gave his patient full attention during the entire birthing room experience, never allowing the irrelevant although delightful activity in the room to distract him from the potential jeopardy inherent in the birthing process.

During my days as a professional aviator, I successfully ejected from a burning military jet aircraft involved in an accident, which required an extensive investigation to find its cause and absolve me of any pilot error. Then, in my civilian medical practice, I delivered a "bad baby," which took a visit to court to find a congenital cause for the malady to absolve me of malpractice. Have you noticed that in life, despite our most conscientious preparation and meticulous conduct, common everyday experiences can ambush us with moments of unforeseen and uncontrollable chaos, leaving no opportunity or time to change their outcomes for good? That is an accident, and an accident by any other name is still an accident.

Insurance companies and attorneys understand otherwise and insist somebody must pay. That is why not just a few medical doctors privately saw the birthing room as tipping the scales away from green-garbed safety and toward the risk of a courtroom. Yet, the pressure of our patient-oriented and consumer-minded culture has a powerful say in the way we dispense medical care despite traditional medicine's unremitting resistance to what it often perceives as less-than-optional practice. Sadly, to this day, well-intentioned people, patients, doctors, and aviators alike sometimes become unwitting victims of unforeseen or out-of-control circumstances as the result of following a road less traveled at the end of which we sometimes discover an unexpected and unwelcome toll booth with a high price to pay.

Ask Jesus if He can relate to that keen observation.

QUESTION: Where is the Kiss from Heaven from this God Story?

ANSWER: On the wall above her little prayer alcove, Emily has a portrait of Jesus in a full state of laughter. It would not be a stretch to claim this God Story as the possible genesis of His hilarious state. It turns me inside out every time I relive this little melodrama. If laughter is a good medicine (Prov. 17:22), then gazing at this Jesus moment is all the healthcare we should ever need. I mentioned that not all childbirths come with pleasant surroundings and lighthearted endings.

Trevor was a beautiful little boy delivered by forceps shortly after our happy tale above. He required neonatal care in several big city hospitals' NICUs (neonatal intensive care units) before a diagnosis of Ondine's curse (central hypoventilation syndrome, a rare congenital condition characterized by failure of an underdeveloped respiratory center in the brain leading to inadequate breathing during sleep) was made. Our local community responded immediately and graciously to a fund drive to help cover Trevor's specialty medical care, first locally and then for a time in a San Francisco hospital. It was a long haul for the little guy, who I spoke to several years ago as an adult raised by his grandparents and now free from any assisted breathing devices. So joyous to know that Trevor won his battle with that cruel nemesis. Even today, I'm guessing Trevor's victory brings joy from Jesus, like that portrait hanging from Emily's wall. What a glorious, although overdue, Kiss from Heaven for the hundreds involved in Trevor's care over the years.

The medical malpractice lawsuit filed by Trevor's financially struggling parents and their ambulance-chasing California lawyer (I'm sorry, but it was sadly my opinion at the time) took a full three years of my life to go nowhere after countless hours of trial preparation, the trial itself, much personal stress, and public humiliation. Jesus more than understood that unfair treatment but, without saying, sans the laughter.

Making Friends (1982)

You could, at one time in history, have crossed the Row River by a bridge about ten miles southeast of Cottage Grove, Oregon, and less than one hundred yards short of its current entrance feeding the upper reaches of Dorena Reservoir. For years, concrete remnants of that long-abandoned bridge had persisted as a border along the river's edge and reminder of times past. On the east side and accessible to a nearby highway was an area open for fishing enthusiasts to park their rigs (often pickups with campers), giving anglers and their families a place to remain overnight during the summer months. It was not an official park but a well-known fishing hole, a hangout for locals, often workers from the Stewart family's mill upriver or loggers who crisscrossed the vast surrounding wilderness during the workweek.

A blazing campfire, tended by chatting moms and younger children, commonly burned throughout the night while dads and older kids fought off the sleep monster to fish from those bridge remnants in forty feet of historic waters from which many a trophy fish had been landed. Largemouth bass taken from the upper reaches of Dorena Reservoir had long ago achieved notoriety in the annals of Oregon's bass fishing lore. Who could be certain what else lurked in those ebony waters bathing that former bridge's final resting place? Stay tuned, Christian.

Kisses from Heaven, Book Three

Looking west from the parking lot at an angle rising thirty degrees, you could glimpse a large home hidden among a cluster of old-growth Douglas firs commanding the top of a steep hillside. Surrounding those mighty trees was a malignant growth of Scotch Broom woven among hordes of piled-high Himalayan blackberry vines. Neither species was indigenous to America, let alone Oregon. As was common elsewhere in our state, over the years, those invaders had jointly formed insurmountable barriers to trespassing on any property they guarded. That included our family's home atop that leveled hilltop three hundred feet west as the osprey flew.

Unsurprisingly, our master bedroom window offered a panoramic view of any enthusiastic group gathered on the riverbank below. Rarely finding time to fish due to an overly busy medical practice, I did, however, discover chances to live vicariously from that bedroom window. The only drawback was the clarity of colorful conversations, laughter, hoots, and hollers well within earshot when a lucky angler was landing another lunker from those foreboding waters. On not an occasional summer's night, the joviality across the way woke us from the soundest slumber. Air conditioning in the home was unnecessary. Breezes off the reservoir through that open master bedroom window were ample substitutes to keep us cool all summer but, I admit, only helped amplify those dark early-morning hour celebrations when fishing was at its best.

Help Me If You Can, I'm Feeling Down

It was a conventional Oregon summer night. Nothing special. Clear. Cool. Comfortable. Only a scattering of folks were fishing from the riverbank, bathed in anemic firelight from a poorly tended fire. Happily, the results were a reduced decibel level and, for us, a welcome diversion from the ordinary and a chance to enjoy deep sleep without interruption. Truth was, like all things good, our precious reverie was about to end. I did not awaken at once. At first, the voices were distant, as if in an inaccessible bad dream. What brought me rudely to the surface and instantly captured my full attention were these words: "Help! Help! We are drowning!" No wonder! By now, serial desperate cries laced with sheer panic filled the open window, flooding our bedroom and hearts with a need to act. Struggling to my feet, I peered outside, trying to locate the source of trouble. It did little good with no moon and minimal help from that night's struggling campfire across the river.

Grabbing my trousers and shoes without socks on the run, within thirty seconds, my 1973 Ford F-250 three-quarter-ton pickup, all 390 V-8 horses kicking gravel from the driveway, found the traction needed to roar downhill toward Government Road. No headlights in sight, the big Ford screeched its way onto the highway to rocket one mile south and the only bridge within reach to cross the waters of the mighty Row.

Regrettably, that also put our rescue effort a mile upstream from tonight's crisis. Submerged beneath the deep black waters of that fishing hole for any time would be problematic. Finding a victim at forty feet during the night would be impossible. That thought made my gut ache. Within a minute, while winging off the highway onto a quarter mile of heavily potholed and puddled dirt path, it was all I could do to keep that big blue behemoth from becoming airborne.

Piling out of the truck near a recently stoked fire surrounded by six people, three wrapped in blankets, I hollered to see if everyone was okay; the answer by all was a resounding, "Yes!" Without solicitation, one angler offered that the three fishermen had rescued the three blanket-wrapped folks from the water with no one the worse for wear. Whoa, what a relief!

Then, an elderly gentleman huddled near the fire and bundled up against the chilly night air stepped forward to share: "My wife, boy, and I arrived about five last evening. We parked the Chevy pickup and camper with its rear door facing the river." Well, I quickly scanned the area for a Chevy pickup with no luck. Nor a camper for a moment. Then, toward the reservoir about forty feet further down the river, in the dim light of the newly fed and now blazing fire, was a camper partially afloat but conveniently in the grip of some outlaw blackberry bushes overflowing the riverbank. Oh my, I was getting the picture.

The old man continued, "At bedtime, my son climbed up to the cab-over bed, my wife stretched out on the dining room table cushions, and I lay down on the floor near the door. We were sound asleep when . . . well, I woke up feelin' the truck creepin' toward the river and 'fore I could do nothin,' we went plumb over that bank. When she hit the water, the back door popped open, and I slid out like a greased pig with Mama in tow. Then, as the truck started sinkin' like a rock, the camper tore off as the rig flat disappeared. The problem was we did not know what happened to the boy. He was nowhere in sight. We were a hollerin' fer help because we thought our son was trapped in the rig and gonna drown . . . or already had. But, just like that, he popped out from the camper's emergency exit, kinda' like a jack-in-the-box on the roof and escaped clean as a whistle. Then the rest of these guys were right there helpin' all of us from the water."

What Now

Wow, what a tale for the grandkids. And how blessed the door had opened for the old man and his wife, and the camper had torn from the truck, or that entire family would have drowned in forty feet of that dark abyss. Instead, all three were safe and sound . . . well, soggy, safe, and sound.

Then the old guy continued, sadly telling the rest of his tale: "That Chevy and our camper are spankin' new today and just off the lot in Springfield. It was my fault. I musta forgot to set the brake or put her in parkin' gear. What now? What now?" The poor old guy looked more than a tad lost, like things were finally catching up, and he was shouldering the burden of it all.

It was only five in the morning with a long day waiting for those folks. So, I offered, "Why don't we head to my place (pointing to the top of the hill), get you all dry clothes, and then breakfast. You can use our telephone and make plans to recover your truck and camper. Then we'll run you back to Springfield."

We Got Lemons, Let's Make Lemonade

Everyone seemed fine with that suggestion, as if there were any other good options. With grateful thanks and good wishes spread around to those alert rescuers, the four of us, stuffed into the front (and only) seat of that bruiser Ford, set out for our place on the rise across the river. Bouncing our way through that muddy trail full of potholes and puddles was an absolute delight for the boy. However, from his parents' silence, the gravity of losing their vehicle and camper while facing a near-life-ending experience, avoided only by their harrowing escapes, seemed to weigh heavily. What could I say? What could anyone say? It was what it was, but for these folks, clearly not at the top of the economic food chain, this fishing trip turned tragedy was a significant setback. I silently thanked the Lord for their safety while praying they had insurance.

Their fourteen-year-old son, I had noted earlier, was a Down's syndrome child who had said nothing of substance since my arrival but now spoke up as we gratefully left the potholes to meet the smoother highway, "Mom and Dad?"

After a moment, his folks put aside their heaviness to answer in unison, "What, son?"

"Well," the young man cheerfully volunteered, "you know, this night has not been all bad."

Again, his folks wrestled for an answer, but this time puzzled, and I sensed a little on edge after the boy's breathtaking comment pretty much sucked all the oxygen out of the cab. "What do you mean by that, son?" his mother asked with a hint of disbelief.

"Well," the little guy responded with genuine delight, "haven't we just made a new friend?"

Oh, my Lord, here came tonight's "Kiss from Heaven," and right on time. Goodness, didn't the love and pride and smiles from the hearts of that elderly couple make their way across the crowded front seat of that now-purring truck like a warm summer breeze. Then, nodding their heads in full agreement, the couple returned their son's smile in spades. In the twinkling of an eye, there had been a weather change in that truck; the sun had risen, chased the clouds away, and brought the light with one life-changing observation from the heart of a fourteen-year-old boy impaired with Down's syndrome. Impairment? No way, not in that truck. "Silent apologies, Lord. Way off track with my earlier thought, wasn't I? These folks are a whole lot richer than I ever imagined." And know what felt so good and warmed my heart to its toes? I saw they already knew it all too well.

Okay, we were home in heartbeats, dried everyone's clothes, filled their tummies with my wife's stout country breakfast, made a few quick phone calls, and whisked them off to Springfield. That now not-so-new Chevy needed a diver and a big-time tow truck to land it as the largest trophy catch ever retrieved from the shadowy depths of that celebrated Row River hole. Then, as a finishing touch, that camper, treading water for the better part of a day, needed a rescue from those riverside outlaw Himalayan blackberry tangles.

Sadly, I never heard from the older couple or the young man again.

Postscript

This comment may seem a tad tangential and a stretch but stick with me. We should not find it difficult, should we, when dealing with humans who differ from us? Oh, but as a fallen human race we do, and in so many ways. Culture, skin color, age, religion, sex, genetic makeup, hair, disability, ideology, wealth, BMR, vocation, beauty, language, behavior, power, prestige, position, politics, talent, ability, intelligence, and—we could go on—stratify us. Differences matter to humans. Diversity matters. Diversity also can make us uncomfortable. And, if you have not noticed by this society's worn-out word "racism," diversity can divide and polarize us.

You ask, "Why aren't we created more alike?" After all, the same unchangeable God has assembled us (Ps. 139:13), and He who is immutable has made us in His image (Gen. 1:26). According to the King James Bible, "He changes not" (Mal. 3:6); then why should we all be so different? Are we meant to be assembly line products or birthed by a cookie cutter? No.

Immutable as God is as an unchangeable living Spirit, He manifests individually and diversely in function as Almighty God and Creator Father, Lord and Savior Son, and Holy Spirit and Companion Helper. As such, we know Him separately but then jointly as the Trinity. Then, immutable as we humans are in our spiritually fallen state (Adamic nature as a product of sin), humankind also manifests itself diversely in unrighteous functions of body (ruling fleshly passions), soul (corrupted mind, rebellious will, and negative emotion), and spirit (dead spirit separated from an unresponsive living God). As such, we are known separately but jointly as sinners, heathen, or lost. However, when acknowledging Jesus the Son as risen Lord and Savior, the broken body and blood of Christ on His Cross of Calvary become a human's full pardon and cleansing from sin (evil doing of body and soul) and death (separation from God in spirit). Then, believing on Him imputes righteousness (right standing before God in body and soul) while our dead spirit is born again and one with His Spirit (1 Cor. 6:19–20).

Immutably one in Spirit with Father God, Jesus, Holy Spirit and one another when born from above, Christians are also made in God's image as unique individuals (even as are Father, Son, and Spirit are in the Trinity), diverse in function (gifts and callings assigned by Holy Spirit for the common good, 1 Cor. 12:11) in the kingdom of Heaven where Father is King, as living stones in the body of Christ where Jesus is King, and in Christian lives where Holy Spirit is King.

Regrettably, through the ongoing pressure of this world's Axis powers, i.e., the spirit of the world (lust of the eyes for carnal power, money, fame, and real estate), lust of the flesh (impure passions and cravings emanating from our fallen Adamic nature), and the boastful pride of life (making room for Satan's lies and his many demonic principalities and spiritual powers, 1 John 2:16), unsaved fallen humans assign one another to divisive groupings, arbitrarily judging and then stratifying those around them as acceptable or not by culture, skin color, age, religion, sex, genetic makeup, disability, interest, ideology, wealth, education, vocation, beauty, language, behavior, power, prestige, position, politics, talents, abilities, intelligence—and we could go on and on (I am doing my best to make a point here by this ongoing, long, run-on sentence).

The Axis powers (world, flesh, and the devil) call the outcome diversity. Then, fallen humanity is compelled to honor and celebrate those diverse groupings according to an ever-changing, politically correct, but morally bankrupt system of arbitrary rankings as the way to unify humankind. So, the Axis tells us to diversify to unify, to emphasize and appreciate our differences as the way to form a perfect union. That is, at the very least, a contradiction and lie of the highest caliber. Let's not denigrate the idea if able to accomplish what it advertises. It does not now and never will. Why? Because diversity is the breeding ground for elitism, prejudice, and discrimination based on judgment, while unity gives birth to equality, respect, tolerance, and acceptance grounded in love.

Observe the Tower of Babel (Gen. 11:7), where God intentionally diversified language to keep people separated, incommunicado, and from unifying as humans bent on challenging His glory. That is correct. God uses diversity to prevent unity, not promote it. He also uses it to shield his glory while the Axis, even to this day, continues efforts to tear down His divine position as God of Heaven and Earth. How reminiscent of Lucifer trying to overthrow the God of Heaven by challenging divine order, distorting the truth, and dividing the foundations (Isa. 14:12–17).

Here, we find a lesson: Darkness never learns from history and always overplays its hand. Look around you; has emphasizing our differences helped draw us together as a unified nation? From 1990, when "Honor Diversity" bumper stickers took hold in Eugene, Oregon, first encouraging, then asking, and finally coercing us to honor diversity by legislation and eventually through the courts, are we more unified as a people? No. Why? True unity never comes by human effort, majority opinion, legislation, judicial ruling, fear of punishment, force, or by emphasizing and honoring differences. Rather, unity is birthed in God's unconditional love by integrating our unique differences, gifts, and callings distributed severally by Holy Spirit (1 Cor. 12:11) as pieces of a magnificent puzzle held together by Christ's unconditional love (Col. 2:8). Remember this: God said from the beginning there is neither Jew or Greek, slave or free, male or female (Gal. 3:28) but all unified as one in Christ.

Everyone who experienced Holy Spirit ministering God's love through that little boy to his troubled parents in my Ford F-250 on that special morning was instantly blessed and unified by God's love. Can you imagine anything conceived on the Axis's socially engineered altar of diversity ever making room for such simple, innocent, and others-centered behavior? It was a miracle, wasn't it, to watch the refreshing wind of His Spirit sweep as a Kiss from Heaven over that crowded pickup burdened by a night's worth of individual sorrows suddenly turned into a morning of unified joy unspeakable and full of glory (Ps. 30:5). Oh, how we underestimate the tender mercies of our God and His ever-present willingness to join with us in our times of trouble. Pick your Kiss from Heaven from this little jewel. You are welcome to share mine.

QUESTION: Where is the Kiss from Heaven from this God Story?

ANSWER: The center of attention after that tragic accident was a fourteen-year-old boy with Down's syndrome. His escape through the overhead hatch of a floating camper torn from the bed of a new Chevrolet pickup sinking into forty feet of dark water settled the fears of his elderly parents treading water and hollering for help nearby. Later, while leaving the scene in my Ford pickup, its front seat crammed with four silent humans, gave the boy's folks time to gain some perspective on that recent event and its financial impact on the family. Curiously, the boy's attention had easily left the accident behind to focus on the wonders of today. What were they? Breaking the silence, the young fella let us know that it had not been an altogether bad day, for they had made a new friend (that would have been yours truly). Today's fearful past event was instantly forgotten while the present suddenly held promise as a person. I wondered if, like that little guy, we could learn to put yesterday's sorrowful tragedies in our rearview mirrors and make today's joyful relationship with Jesus our focus, wouldn't He make our hard times give way to the better? Didn't that question instantly become moot when the sweet wind of Holy Spirit suddenly began to blow as an unsolicited Kiss from Heaven across the front seat of that bruiser Ford all the way to Mom feeding us a stout country breakfast a stone's throw up the hill from the mighty Row River feeding her reservoir.

A Black Cloud (1983)

Oregon is well known for 49 of its original 450 covered bridges still in service. About one-half were open for vehicle use in 2024, with the remaining relegated to "tourist status" alongside their newer modern steel or concrete replacements. Using lumber, the Beaver State's most economic staple and least expensive building material, to erect both covered highway and railway bridges across waterways coursing the state was standard procedure for the better part of the last century. Protecting bridges from the harsher environmental elements by covering and siding these structures added up to seventy years to their useful lives. Maintaining the bridges' driving surfaces, like those found on boardwalks and early plank roads elsewhere in the country, presented a challenge to safely using the elderly bridges carrying vehicle traffic. Although replaceable, the planking eventually became worn, smooth, occasionally rotted, and devoid of purchase when subjected to wet or icy conditions. Making matters more treacherous, an imperceptible mold that flourishes outside direct sunlight during the cooler and wetter times of year negatively affected traction. That situation worsened when accumulation of grease, oil, and gasoline residue from day-to-day vehicle use reduced a tire's grip further. In 1983, Oregon was gradually replacing wooden bridges. A number, however, had remained in full-time service. The Currin Bridge over the Row River in Lane County was one of those.

Destiny's Ride

The Currin covered bridge was built to carry Layng Road west to east across the Row River to dead-end in a perpendicular entrance to Row River Road, which runs north and south alongside the river itself. Built by Lane County in 1925, that 105 feet of wooden bridge served as an alternate route to and from my office in Cottage Grove and our home on Dorena Reservoir for ten years.

For years, the asphalt roadbed abutting the bridge's western entrance rose at an angle abrupt enough to catapult any swiftly moving vehicle heading east into a near-zero-gravity condition before landing upon its well-worn planks. The children always welcomed this historically innocent and playful "whoop-dee-doo" maneuver for the way it cemented their tummies to the old Suburban's ceiling with a second or two of negative G's. So, late one soggy autumn afternoon, while being motivated by the children's cheers of encouragement, I launched Big Brown into a brief negative-G state from that elevated and slippery west entryway onto the waiting bridge. Instantly, slowing down became a problem as the Suburban slithered and slid its way along the greasy bridge surface within the tight limits of its enclosed walls. Having spent years of icy winters in the Northeast, I judiciously "milked" the brakes repeatedly to seek intermittent traction, avoid total loss of control, and reduce speed. It did no good. The Brown Bomber was still pushing twenty-five miles an hour when we exited the 105-foot span, less than a stone's throw of wet asphalt before the road's end and a stop sign guarding the entrance to an equally wet and leave-strewn Row River Road.

Straight ahead, across that busy highway, lay a deep ditch denying access to a fenced farmer's field. Suddenly, I was less concerned about engaging both that ditch, fence, and field as I was brazenly intersecting the path of a ponderous and overloaded Peterbilt log truck only yards to the south and relentlessly bearing down upon our projected position at an excessive rate of speed. The log truck had no chance of slowing on that wet, leaf-strewn, slick country road, and that meant, if the Suburban did not quickly come to a complete halt, there would be a violent collision and tragic loss of life. There is an inflexible given that every Oregonian understands: No vehicle contests a loaded Oregon log truck and wins.

Careening down the decline, leaving the bridge toward the intersection, I continued to furiously seek the purchase from that uncooperative brief stretch of wet asphalt. In my peripheral vision, I caught the stop sign sliding by as the Suburban violated the sanctity of the main highway while at the same moment catching my second daughter shrink fearfully into her terror-laden "suicide seat" from the corner of my eye. Never will I forget how my gut ached as this scene unfolded, one prolonged nanosecond after another. At the exact instant that Big Brown slid to his indecisive halt before the path of that Peterbilt colossus, that same menacing truck, overflowing the entire expanse of Brown's windshield with its titanic presence, swept by scant inches from the Suburban's grill with air horns blaring like the out-of-control locomotive it had become.

Abruptly, there was this eerie, contradictory silence. The day's big event was over, but for that Peterbilt's backwash, a dervish of wet leaves silently settling as an offensive memory upon Big Brown's glass, and hearts pounding in the ears of all. While my children will never forget that near-fatal incident, the bridge on Layng Road would, from then on, stand as a landmark to my recklessness as a father. Without saying, that moment also proved the goodness of God in the land of the living (Ps. 27:13), where Jesus confirmed Himself, once again, as Savior with a most extraordinary Kiss from Heaven.

An Avian Eclipse

Autumns later, a temporary weather break produced an unexpected but welcome change from the dull gray, dreary, drizzly, and droning-on-and-on climate patterns so typical of the southern Willamette Valley entering winters during the 1980s. Following our family's move to Oregon, we rarely, if ever, saw the sun from September of that first year to June of the next. There is a measure of truth in the axiom that Oregonians rust out before they wear out. Blissfully happy people often moved from California during an exquisite Oregon summer only to sacrifice their new homes to the rain gods (often confused with realtors) by February of the following year as an impractical but lone choice to return south and refurbish their lives with sunshine, warm weather, and freedom from Prozac.

All those high-intensity light parlors designed to treat seasonal affective disorder (a depressive mood condition brought on by a prolonged lack of direct sunlight) did not thrive in Oregon by mistake, my friend. To have any moments of intrusion by Old Sol, broken clouds, or even high overcasts in an Oregon winter was worth a king's ransom when imprisoned beneath those morose skies while awaiting an infinitely distant summer.

Homeward Bound

So, there were Big Brown and yours truly, sloshing our way home late one Thursday afternoon when the heavens inexplicably parted, leaving but few clouds even at altitude. Heading south on Row River Road to once again face that Currin Bridge memory, I glanced across the ditch guarding those expansive farmer fields to the east, hoping to glimpse the Three Sisters, a trilogy of large snow-capped peaks in the remote Cascade Mountain Range. Often visible from our site under ideal conditions, today, an enormous black cloud overshadowed those peaks, obliterating the entire horizon and moving slowly toward our position. What was going on? Parking Big Brown, what had been a puzzle cleared. That approaching black cloud was geese, hundreds of thousands of Canadian geese on yearly migration. Never, even as a hunter, had I seen such massive flights of these disciplined birds at once. Like squadron after squadron of the US Army Air Force's B-17 flying fortresses pressing toward ill-fated German cities in World War II, countless V-shaped formations of those giant Canadians soon overshadowed our position, blacking out the blue sky overhead as might a solar eclipse.

The Invitation

Oh, the bedlam pouring from the innumerable thousands of geese honking in unison overhead. On and on, they relentlessly came. Within an hour, the sky to the east began to gradually restore light to the darkened day while the din continued until the last flights were within a half mile. Only then did the decibel level measurably go down. At that moment, I noticed a change not only in the intensity of the noise but in its origin. Somehow, I was hearing this racket in stereo. Strange!

Tuning in more carefully, there was no doubt that the honking was coming not only from the heavens but also from somewhere on Earth. Walking the highway approaching my ever-present "bridge over troubled waters" and the reliable invasive memories of that never-distant "near miss," I made a discovery. Across the river, strewn about the lawn of a riverfront home, were a half-dozen Canadian geese frantically extending their necks aloft, vigorously flapping their wings, and honking for all they were worth. Altogether worked up, these birds were engaged in a powerful process by the goings-on overhead. The more they honked, the more enthusiastic they became. The more they flapped their wings, the closer they came to taking flight. Something powerful was challenging these magnificent birds. Was it an invitation? Were they facing a monumental decision?

Thinning remnants of the migration continued to stream overhead but in steadily reduced numbers. Within minutes, even the stragglers disappeared while fewer and fewer isolated calls came from a distance. At the river's edge, the "domesticated" Canadian geese had settled down to occasional honks accompanied by isolated wing flaps. Finally, all activity ended under a vacant sky. The world had again become blissfully quiet. In that solitary moment, the Lord spoke to my spirit in a still, small, but penetrating voice: "Many are called, but few are chosen" (Matt. 22:14). That was it.

Postscript

So, had I understood the Lord to say the vast multitude flooding the heavens for over an hour were the chosen "few"? Did our sky recently teeming with birds turning our day into night represent the "few" and not the "many"? That was bewildering. If these geese represented the "few," then who were the "many"? Suddenly, I understood: Six geese here and six geese there on earth refusing an invitation by those on a mission overhead seeking them to press into their destinies. Six geese here and six geese there, totaling millions along the migration route, hearing but resisting that clarion call.

But why the resistance? Hadn't the geese on the neighbor's lawn seemed enthusiastic, energized, and excited? Hadn't they known this was an invitation to something grand, much larger than themselves, and altogether life-changing? All they needed to join the quest was a desire to go where they were meant to go, do what they were meant to do, and become what they were meant to be. In the passion of the moment, all this primal logic seemed clear to each one's inner goose, didn't it?

Something deep within was stirring them to go, to do, and to become. But the invitation never seemed enticing enough, nor the call strong enough to overcome deep but hidden reservations. It was not as if they could not respond; they were, instead, simply unwilling.

Somehow, those geese found themselves attached to their surroundings. They had chosen the "things" of earth (safety, shelter, food, ease, and comfort) over the "things" above (their destiny: to go, to do, and to become).

Could geese become attached to the "things" of this world? Seems they had, first wanting, then needing, and next expecting those "things"—until insisting on them. Addicted to guaranteed security, finest shelter, choicest food, uninterrupted ease, and sustained comfort, they came to fear insecurity, homelessness, hunger, labor, and pain. The "things of this world" were no longer options; they were necessities. Expectations were to be promptly fulfilled as entitlements, demands instantly satisfied, indulgences endlessly gratified, and delicacies unceasingly consumed. And on and on.

Where might those geese have traveled, what they might have done, and who they might have become would thereafter be a mystery. Although called, they chose not to be chosen. They could never again claim to be powerless victims of their environment, circumstances, or even of another's behavior because they had tasted the opportunity, evaluated the call, and rejected it.

Nothing had hindered them but their own self-will. That alone determined their choice to reject the call and seal their destiny. From now on, there would be no more struggles. They had succumbed to the "things" of this world. They would go nowhere else, do nothing more, and become no more than their present world demanded. That one flyover had exposed the condition of their resistant, reprobate, and self-indulgent hearts. There would be no turning back; with their decision to remain among the "many," they excluded themselves from the "few."

With that mindset, the faintest whisper of any lingering call faded like the fragrance of a flower pressed dead in an album of forgotten memories and unfulfilled dreams. And miles to the west, the "few," spreading their invitations, all Kisses from Heaven, flew on.

Oh, that it be not too late for us, Christians, to heed the central evangelical lesson of the Canadian goose: The opportunity of a lifetime lasts only as long as the lifetime of the opportunity, a Kiss from Heaven from a God who has "plans for prosperity and not for harm, plans to give you a future and a hope" (Jer. 29:11).

QUESTION: Where is the Kiss from Heaven from this God Story?

ANSWER: Do you have places on this earth that conjure up significant memories? You know, places that elicit warm fuzzy feelings or unspeakable dread? Are you ready? Then I ask you this: How many times have you been out of control in a dreaded slide over 159 short feet of greasy, intractable roadway in a Chevy Suburban load of children paralyzed by fear on a direct course to intersect 80,000 pounds of blaring Peterbilt log truck loaded with giant Douglas firs traveling at fifty miles per hour on a rainswept Row River Road, only to come up short by a mere twenty-four inches? You would remember too, wouldn't you? Only the last two feet of this tale was a Kiss from Heaven. Earlier? One-hundred-fifty-seven feet straight from hell. As an aviator, I might have mindlessly quipped, "Any landing you walk away from is a good landing." As a born-again Christian dad, it became, "Praise you, my eleventh-hour, fifty-nine minute, and fifty-nine-second Jesus for this undeserved Kiss from Heaven."

10

A Mid-Afternoon Snooze (1983)

Autumn runs my motor. Part of it comes from my youth and pheasant hunting with my dad, sandlot football with my friends, and a blazing maple leaf canopy enveloping our street in Upstate New York. Then there were crisp Macintosh apples snatched from an abandoned orchard near home, the phosphorous white harvest moons, bone-chilly nights, and warm, sun-drenched days.

The latter caused me, as a middle-aged man, to abruptly change my destination that Thursday afternoon while motoring in Western Oregon toward the Bohemia Mountains in quest of my weekly respite. Fatigued from an entire night's vigil hovering over a grindingly slow labor, what I needed most was a nap and that sooner than later. Abbreviating the trip by plunging through a stand of Douglas firs pierced by the first logging road to come along, the Toyota half-ton laden with its mini camper, desperately grasping for traction from the steep and deeply rutted ancient hillside trail, finally came to an abrupt but welcome halt on an abandoned landing formerly used to load old-growth logs onto giant trucks bound for the mill upriver.

Grabbing my Bible, I pushed into the dense forest covering the steep mountainside. Not soon enough, a small knoll leveled out ahead into a flat patch of sun-flooded, leaf-strewn ground tailor-made for a nap. I crashed into the leaf pile, settled onto my back, hands laced together behind my head, and went straight to dreamland under that warm autumn sun.

When we look directly into Old Sol with closed eyes, can you recall how bright things appear until something blocks the light? Well, that's what happened. At least, I thought so, having been briefly awakened when something seemed to extinguish the sunlight. One thing was certain: Having no interest in ending my coveted nap, I intentionally slipped back into slumber only to be awakened again by that same puzzling phenomenon.

Eyelids tightly closed while desperately trying to preserve my drowsy state behind them, I analyzed the possibilities for these rude interruptions. There could be a tree swaying in the wind and intermittently blocking the sunlight. That I eliminated; there was no palpable wind. Could there be a deer grazing nearby? Highly unlikely. How about something a little more formidable, like a bear, a big cat, or even a wolf? Coming across the latter three in these wild places over the years, all would be unlikely candidates if only for the fear they held for men. Still, anything was possible. With that thought, I had another: Was I about to meet yet another angel? Before I could process that question, there was that shadow again, this time with an unidentifiable noise. What was going on? It was becoming creepy; understandably, I was now wide awake behind those sealed lids.

Simultaneously breaking into a squint without moving a muscle, the apparition at that instant eclipsed the sunlight. Throwing my eyes wide open, the afternoon brightness smacked my retinas, forcing my lids to involuntarily close for seconds. Finally, wide-eyed but still as a stone while scanning my surroundings, difficult while lying on my back, I found nothing out of the ordinary to solve this mounting mystery.

Then, a shadow raced across the firs bordering my resting place and quickly disappeared. Then, without warning, three feet before my eyes and briefly looming overhead like a B-52 on a low-level bombing run was a form that caused a little chill down my back, followed by a surge of adrenaline in my gut. As quickly out of sight as it had appeared, I wondered, "What will be its next move?" Predictably, and within seconds, another apparition swept by, merely inches from my face, and, this time, confirming my suspicion.

As soon as the scepter vanished, I rolled to a prone position and looked behind me; there was the rest of the unsavory squadron leaving their downwind leg and entering their final approach. On they came, boldly and unafraid, on and on until I could not wait another heartbeat. By now, supremely overconfident that their landing zone was secure, nothing would deter them from the carnage to follow. In a nanosecond, and to their complete surprise, I leaped to my feet. Wasn't I hearing them cry in a helter-skelter sequence, "Fouled deck, fouled deck! Wave off, wave off, wave off."

The division leader first flirted precariously with a stall while avoiding my head while his wingman performed a nifty high-G maneuver in an emergency climb to altitude. The following squadron members instantly peeled off in many directions, banking sharply and adding full power to separate themselves from danger.

Within moments, it was over. All was still. The threat, imposing as it was, was now not. No longer targeted as tonight's blue plate special, I could resume my nap. The turkey buzzards were gone, and my postponed Kiss from Heaven was in hand.

Postscript

This short-lived laboratory experience reminds me of an important life lesson: The quickest and most effective way to dispel invasions by unwanted interlopers is to first wake up and then stand up. Most bullies back down even with casual resistance. However, a large contingent of us would rather avoid discomforting conflicts by closing our eyes, looking the other way, or taking real or, at the very least, metaphorical naps. Historically, negotiation to fend off conflict merely sets up thirty-eighth parallels, DMZs, or cold wars, which let the buzzards circle indefinitely, even if they intend not to land. Humans entrenched in comfort of the status quo will do nearly anything outside physical aggression to obviate distressful or sacrificial action. The prospect of pain and loss intimidates contented people, tempting them to close their eyes and dive further under the covers. Wars happen not so much because nations readily stand up for themselves but because they do not. Peace-loving people groups throughout history have kept their eyes closed, denied the ominous approach of evil, and only when forced by an enemy (who had decided that their foe was dead or dying) finally stood up for themselves. Too often, they found, too late.

The irony remains that peaceful nations end in war to keep their peace because they do not aggressively draw a "line in the sand" earlier on. By the time they face new, radical, and idealistic barbarians at or within their gates, they themselves have regrettably become entrenched, recalcitrant, self-indulgent, money-grubbing elitists and cowards welcoming them. Is this speaking to you like it's speaking to me? So, again, it is not so much how others treat us that decides our destinies but how soon and how effectively we respond to their treatment. Every wise parent understands that early intervention nips improper behavior in the bud, sets the tone for future encounters, and keeps parenting skills honed to readiness.

Does that mean that world history, wise parenting, or even those turkey buzzards have taught us something here? Not necessarily. Consider the snooze alarm!

QUESTION: Where is the Kiss from Heaven from this God Story?

ANSWER: Well, wasn't it a Kiss from Heaven that those buzzards weren't Pelagornis sandersi?*

*The prehistoric Pelagornis sandersi had an estimated wingspan of twenty-four feet, making it the largest known flying carnivorous creature of all time. Well, not so wide as the Russian Antonov An-225, an aircraft that looks like a creature, has a wingspan of 290 feet, and a carnivorous appetite for jet fuel (which conceivably may have been distilled over the eons from the remains of a multitude of Pelagornis sandersi and their prehistoric cronies transformed to oil deep within the earth—or not).

11

In the Heart of Darkness (1984)

Our team had not been at sea level for weeks. The refreshing and sweet fragrances carried by those Mindanao Mountain breezes rapidly became a memory as stifling heat and oppressive humidity greeted us in the Philippine lowlands. This was a Mississippi summer on steroids and not the warm welcome we would have chosen. Upon reaching our destination, an acknowledged stronghold of the vicious New Peoples' Army Communist insurgency, our leaders reminded us of that danger. Most took this reminder as a caution, while my history as a combat Marine embraced it more like DEFCON 2.

Etched in my mind was the carnage and loss of life following that rebel ambush of a packed civilian bus we stumbled upon on the first day of our journey weeks ago. That mindless slaughter of innocents and rebels thrust into our path, I had taken in a simplistic way: We were in a war zone. So, as of today, we had entered the enemy's command and control center, breaching what I saw as the heart of darkness.

It was hardly a surprise that the crumbling, aged three-storied structure before us, a remnant of the former iron-fisted days of Spanish totalitarian rule of the Philippines, raised the hairs on the back of my neck. With a flat roof and three levels of rusted ornate balconies crisscrossing its stern face, the unpainted wooden relic was eerily reminiscent of those elderly mansions frequenting Charles Adam's New Yorker cartoons of decades past. Approaching its looming presence, I could easily imagine elegant Spanish ladies with shining black hair piled high over beautiful bare-backed red dresses fanning themselves seductively before debonaire suitors serenading from the street below or, as readily, the building bustling as a busy bordello frequented by sailors from the powerful Spanish fleet anchored in the bay nearby.

Fantasy completed and climbing the narrow stairway exiting the kitchen, I noticed an antique wood cook stove pressed firmly against a tinder-dry wall, longing to embrace an errant well-placed spark. We would lodge on the second floor. Little chance of a good night's sleep tonight in this firetrap. Prophetic, I tell you.

Our evangelical team occupied spacious but separate sleeping areas distinguished from boot camp barracks only by the absence of "double-decker" bunks. Rows of beds stretched from wall to wall while giant gaping windows looked to capture every errant breeze blowing off the nearby saltwater bay became a welcome but scant relief from the oppressive heat of this tropical afternoon. It was not long before three of us were strolling beneath the blazing sun, over pure white sands, and recklessly wading through clear azure waters. As quickly, we found ourselves gathered about a makeshift "operating" table, laboriously removing countless sea urchin spines from the foot of one of our distressed colleagues. Was this to be a harbinger of things to come? Tonight's crusade in a local soccer stadium was an unknown. Over the last weeks, God had met native Filipinos hungry for the Lord in various settings. Why should this night be different? I had my reasons.

Preparing

Hours before the meeting, we gathered for intercessory prayer. Heaviness had settled with the deepening twilight over our gathering. This heart of darkness was affecting, even contaminating, the atmosphere of our prayer time. Listening to our leaders describe what I, too, was feeling, oppression laced with anxiety caused my knees to weaken.

Mercifully, while they conversed, the Lord called me to my face in prayer to intercede for the upcoming meeting with a passion I had never experienced. During this brief but intense interval, He opened my eyes to a vivid, lifelike inner vision. Moving through the heavens from my right to left, endless legions of angels in bright, shining armor and riding muscular pure white steeds advanced above me. Following the cavalry came foot soldiers, huge and powerful warriors, brilliantly clad in white and marching rhythmically as if to an unseen drummer. What an awe-inspiring and fearsome sight. Banners unfolded, these warring angels were focusing on and preparing for battle. Like a giant, my spirit arose within me. How could this heart of darkness prevail before the might and power of the Lord's army? The team rejoiced as our corporate spirits lightened. We felt ready.

Entering the Heart of Darkness

In a decaying town with little to no street lighting, we felt our way through dark back alleyways before finally filing into a run-down soccer stadium rimmed by dented sheets of corrugated steel, heavily rusted about their scars and covered with graffiti. Wandering forward to a makeshift stage erected before as hostile a group as I had ever seen in a peacetime setting, we all recognized that the war was on. The light source, single incandescent bulbs powered by an ancient struggling generator, was inadequate to appreciate the row after row of dirty, grim-faced men, arrogantly brandishing AK-47 automatic weapons, and soon enough eager to challenge our evangelist's every word.

As the meeting progressed, what small light emitted from those few bare bulbs above cast long, inconsistent shadows over the morose crowd with each power surge. Repeatedly, the huge speakers, at first deafening, then alternately screeching, scratching, or screaming, finally failed altogether before inexplicably exploding back to life.

The gospel message was incoherent, causing the unsettled crowd to become visibly restless and increasingly hostile. It was understandable; our evangelist was preaching a mighty God to these men with no god outside communism, men who were taught that religion was the opium of the masses, there was no Christian God, and that Christians were enemies of their cause. That observation had never been more real than at that moment when the covert rage of our audience spilled over into foul words and mockery.

Mind and body on full military alert and as tense as the situation had become, there simultaneously arose in me an almost inappropriate paradox, a sadness and compassion for those hardened, cold, wounded, and deceived men so willfully ignoring a loving God while blindly and enthusiastically embracing their Marxist demon.

The meeting was unraveling and about to break up way before expected. The tension in the gathering was palpable with no police presence in sight. We were at the mercy of this unstable mob, and their hostility was reaching critical mass. Without hesitation, our leaders, leaving the stage, motioned us to follow. Riveted on the exit, we retraced our steps while becoming ready targets for the disparaging remarks from the seething and vocal crowd. Escaping the enclosure, we hurriedly sought separation from our antagonists, losing ourselves deep within the town before, hours later, finally groping our way back to our quarters through the darkness.

A No-Nonsense Night

There was not a soul among us who did not long for a good night's sleep or to vacate this ancient firetrap at first light. The town had not been ready for us, and had it not been for Heaven's warring angels, we would not have been ready for it. (Parenthetically, I am convinced that the Apostle Paul may have found this a relaxing night. Comparing ourselves with ourselves, we were genuinely happy not to be stoned and left for dead, given thirty-nine lashes, thrown into prison or, more likely, found by the working end of an AK-47.) Gratefully thanking Jesus for our angels' help, I fell asleep in a heartbeat, only to wake to shrieks and commotion coming from the women's dormitory in the wee hours of the morning.

It was still dark when a large bat (Filipino fruit bats grow to wingspans of 1.8 meters) found entrance to their quarters. In the confusion that followed, a lighted oil lamp inadvertently fell from a table to set the floor ablaze. In the furious attempts to quench the flames, the whole room came to life while the bat went its merry way unnoticed. Within minutes, the women extinguished the fire. How close had we come to fulfilling my firetrap prophecy?

When Enough Was Not Enough

If that early-morning incident was not enough to encourage our prompt departure, here is the story our leaders shared with the team about their encounter during the previous night's watch. Understand this is secondhand information and hearsay; I remember the story, however, as if shared over this morning's coffee. Here is why: Everyone was fast asleep when both leaders woke in unison to a raucous, large, heavily armed, torch-bearing mob touting communist banners and singing revolutionary songs from the street before our hacienda.

Over a blaring bullhorn, its leader challenged us to come debate him while mocking our cowardice for not doing so. He steadfastly continued this rhetoric while our leaders wisely stayed in the shadows and beyond sight. Our pastor prayed that the Lord would impart a deep sleep to our team. Gratefully, not one other soul heard a sound that night. Despite all the clamor and threats from the menacing mob, which refused to be resigned to our unwillingness to enter their arena, the communist rebels withdrew while singing their "patriotic" songs until they were out of earshot.

Angels on Assignment

Listening to their tale, my mind went once again to that vision of countless warrior angels coming to our rescue. Always vigilant, for the second time in eight hours, they marshaled their forces to hold a vengeful mob at bay. There was no chance for us to have resisted either that seething bunch at the evening's meeting or last night's zealots had they stormed that old Spanish building while we slept.

Had our angels had enough for one day? Likely. They enjoyed those challenges and may have even wished for more. Warriors do that, you know. Still, rather than test them or God, we hurriedly gathered up our belongings, scurried past that unlit wood stove, loaded our vehicles, and made a swift departure. Were we retreating? Absolutely. No one felt the need to justify our retreat but only to do so. Besides, that battle had always belonged to the Lord and His angels. After those big guys stomped darkness into submission twice in one day, would another defeat of a twice-defeated foe hold any interest for them? Would make little sense to this man, but then, I am no angel.

I also wondered on our way out of town if those impressive warriors were expected to multitask (a concept without a name, I might add, in the 1980s). It was not beyond reason that the gospel may have pricked the heart of a confirmed Marxist at the previous evening's meeting. A ministering angel would then have had to reach out, embrace, strengthen, and comfort that new convert as an heir of salvation

(Heb. 1:14). Have you considered this assignment, a perfect fit for a spiritual nursemaid, might have pushed those big warrior guys over the edge? I had to smile thinking about it. Not long enough, however, to watch it.

Postscript

Remember how the Apostle Peter, surreptitiously released from jail by an angel, was not welcomed by an unbelieving group of believers in the book of Acts (Acts 1:15)? In defense of their faith or, rather, the lack of it, we are commonly hesitant to embrace miraculous interventions as solutions to recalcitrant real-life dilemmas, at least without first seeking logical explanations. Mercifully overlooking our unbelief, the Lord often quietly directs His unseen angels to turn things around at the last minute to spare His children from menacing storms that come in the dark nights of their lives. Angels, as you can see, tend not to showboat. Does this stuff happen, and we are simply not privy to it? After that night, I am a believer.

When a reliable friend shared a tale of his elderly parents standing in their Oklahoma kitchen window watching a monster tornado uproot a 100-year-old cottonwood tree the size of a silo from their side yard as the twister squeezed itself between an enormous barn full of expensive horses and their own stately and historic farmhouse, it is easy to default to words like "good luck" or "good karma." Can't we as easily imagine a giant angel, or even our "good God" Himself, stuffing a big finger into the top of that funnel cloud to move it from the path of a confused and dangerously exposed elderly couple and a whole bunch of spooked horses? As Christians, why not?

Okay, to be fair, if you are the 10 percent who are more focused on and environmentally grieved over that tornado taking a prized cottonwood tree the size of a silo, then you have never had to spring clean a yard with a cottonwood tree the size of a silo. When we lose a squatter like that to the voracious gullet of a monster twister, we should consider it an environmental miracle, i.e., no more days of spring cleaning and nights full of leg cramps, hot baths, and Doan's pills. Having clearly understood, late that afternoon, that legions of angels had been assigned to protect us in the heart of darkness, it was easy for me to accept those majestic heavenly beings as the Lord's most recent Kisses from Heaven, who led us to a premature departure from that volatile soccer stadium meeting, guided us through the dark, unfamiliar recesses of the town to the safety of our quarters, and gave us sweet sleep and protection before that aggressive mob during the night. Then, in the early-morning hours, they helped the women extinguish the sudden early-morning fire in their sleeping quarters, chased the bat away, and, finally, ensured our hurried withdrawal from that dark city.

Having not had an inner vision so vivid since I saw those heavenly warriors during that time of intercessory prayer so many years ago, is it surprising that I have not been overly nostalgic nor desperately in need to join those heavenly beings in similar surroundings since?

Why? Simple. How about "You shall not tempt the Lord your God" (Matt. 4:7). Amen.

QUESTION: Where is the Kiss from Heaven from this God Story?

ANSWER: In this God Story, there are competing Kisses from Heaven. Walking away with our lives from that demon-infested soccer stadium bristling with seething AK-47 carrying communist New People's Army foot soldiers and later their threatening late-night visit to our sleeping quarters head the list . . . closely followed by a bigger-than-life inner vision of mighty legions of shining angelic cavalry and powerful infantry as a second round of kisses and the likely reasons we escaped that stadium and firetrap to begin with.

♥ 12

The Number Two Elevator (1984)

The number two elevator had become wedged between the second and third floors of the Midtown Hotel in downtown Manilla two years earlier, abruptly interrupting an express descent to the lobby and throwing the packed car into a state of high anxiety. Trapped in an unlit, overflowing black box without air conditioning, an already steaming tropical afternoon unsettled the best of us, even those with no history of claustrophobia. Pressed against the locked door when the elevator came to its sudden stop, there was a brief hush where no one spoke for seconds until my companions began to pray aloud in the Spirit. That sent a shockwave through the paralyzed car, jumpstarting murmurs and finally provoking one Filipino gentleman sequestered somewhere toward the back of that packed sardine can to cry out, "Stop that!" Wouldn't we have wagered him an unbeliever who saw no connection between that prayer and our elevator's immediate resumption of its routine journey to deliver an entire load of relieved passengers safely to the first floor.

Two years later, when my eldest daughter, Melanie, and I entered the hotel, checked in, and sought an elevator to the fourteenth floor, the number two car was again out of service. How could I not help chuckle within? Having a history with that number two elevator and seeing it disabled again triggered that distant memory. Then, I wondered if that unit had been out of service for the entire two-year interval. Unlikely but possible. Hey, we were in Asia.

The following day, Melanie and I returned to the hotel from town and, mindlessly, I admit, took the number two car, assumed to be fresh from its shakedown cruise and returned to service. All other passengers had disembarked by the twelfth floor, leaving the two of us alone on our ascent. Moving closer to the doors and expecting a short journey to the fourteenth floor, weren't we surprised when the car bypassed our selected stop and continued an upward climb. Passing the fifteenth floor, I pushed the button to the sixteenth, which the car ignored as it flew by on its seemingly relentless journey. But to where and how was this possible? Repeatedly using the "Emergency Stop" button to no avail, I ended by indiscriminately pressing every button in sight, all without a hint of a response from any. Then, with a mind-boggling, bone-rattling, knee-buckling shock, the elevator ran out of shaft, assumably by striking the highest point available. Bouncing off an obstacle hidden somewhere beyond our car's ceiling tiles, the rogue car began an improbable cycle of assaulting that unseen obstacle, backing off to batter it again and then again and again. Within, both of us held on for dear life while trying to keep our footing as the convulsing car continued its unrelenting suicidal behavior. All my ongoing attempts to press those buttons continued to meet with no response and with cell phones yet a fantasy, there were no means to seek the hotel's help. Nothing was working! Nothing!

Finally, in a desperate move to seek egress, I struggled with all my strength to pry the elevator doors apart, only to reveal a furiously oscillating solid brick wall blocking all escape. We were trapped! Despite my repeated attempts to suppress it, Edgar Allen Poe's short story, "The Cask of Amontillado" and the tragic end met by its primary character kept flooding my mind.

Praying, whether aloud or in silence, I cannot recall, here I was with my first child, a daughter I had asked along on this journey expressly to draw us closer. Would my well-intentioned invitation lead to her death? The elevator could not keep up this incessant self-imposed abuse forever; mechanically, one part or another eventually failed. Would that mean plunging twenty floors together to unite our lives forever by some unspoken macabre Hollywood-like suicidal death pact? Were we now in a horrifying drama with cameras withdrawing from a hopeless final scene where both innocent protagonists had exhausted all means of escape, only to fade into a desperate but impossible fight to stay alive?

With one final heroic thrust to seek freedom from its unyielding adversary, the captive car, somehow breaking loose its bonds, suddenly began a freefall, instantly accelerating downward in a negative-G, uncontrollable, and terrifying silence. But to what end? Well to a Kiss from Heaven, another incredible knee-bending but briefest of stops at the eighteenth floor, where we gratefully stumbled from the car's clutches before it continued its carefree descent. Shaken but happily wobbling downstairs to the fourteenth floor, we hastily telephoned the front desk to report the incident.

Leaving the building that evening, elevator number two was once more out of service. A good riddance, I thought; change can be slower than molasses in January in the Philippine culture. Indisputably, that included maintenance for the all-too-predictably-unpredictable number two elevator now enjoying another unscheduled break (pardon the pun) at the Midtown Hotel in downtown Manila.

Postscript

As a creator of sorts who loves to design, build, and then move on has been my strength. Maintenance, however, has never pushed my buttons (oh, isn't "pushed my buttons" still a provocative trigger). Day-to-day surveillance, tweaking an object to keep it running smoothly, and repairing something that has worked without interruption or attention for years makes me weary. It feels that after all the extra time, effort, and money spent in getting the thing up and running in the first place, the thing should have enough respect and without the gall to break down in the second. Should the thing not have responsibility to carry its own load?

You can see why my 1984 Toyota's engine gave up the ghost after ninety-thousand miles without a single oil change (I know) and my first marriage tanked after twenty-five years for analogous reasons (I know, I know). Anyway, thankfully, I have profited from my past mistakes by changing the car's oil every three thousand miles (using synthetics protects a whole lot longer if you want some insurance), watching over my second wife, sweet Emily, of twenty-seven years by keeping our date nights, and renewing our vows every five years to make sure Jesus continues as captain of our love boat. After the Toyota required a new engine, the marriage (after an eleven-year interval), a new bride, and, to be transparent, a couple of hiccoughs in my relationship with Heaven needed restoration, I have at least learned the basics.

Speaking of Heaven, doesn't our relationship with Jesus require maintenance also? Now, He is the creator of all things, right (John 1:3)? And He holds all things together, right (Col. 1:17)? But who gets to do the routine day-to-day maintenance? How do we play our part in deepening our relationship with the Lord? Or tweak it to keep it running smoothly? What happens when there is a catastrophic breakdown analogous to an engine failure in a Toyota or an unfixable obstacle in a teetering marriage? What about a significant backslide in our faith walk itself?

Folks talk of an eternally secure relationship with Christ and then end the conversation. That makes me wince. Come on now; the promises of God often require our participation. If we cannot wait to turn ninety thousand miles on the Toyota or twenty-five years in a marriage, can we even wait twenty-four hours to tend to our relationship with the Lord? Think about who we are ignoring here.

Smith Wigglesworth, the immensely popular English evangelist, would go on afternoon walks with friends following Sunday dinners. All reported that he would pause regularly during their conversations, step aside, and ask the Lord if He would like to contribute anything to the group chat before moving on. Then, remember how Jesus rose early each morning to seek a lonely place to spend time with his Father? He kept the relationship by communication so tuned to Heaven that, the Scriptures say, He never spoke or did anything He did not hear the Father speak or see the Father do (John 12:49). That had to take serious time. Then there was Jesus' brother, James, who spent so much time with Father in prayer that the early church dubbed him "Old Camel Knees," referring to the callouses attending James's joints.

So, may studying our Bibles help? Knowing about Jesus is a good thing. What about going to church? Fellowshipping with the saints is essential to pleasing the Lord. And giving to the poor? Sacrificial giving is an excellent way to minister to Jesus. However, the Bible supports and even commands more.

Are these actions enough to support an intimate love relationship with our Savior? Honestly, I do not believe so much as we might wish. Little more than reading the Toyota manual brings about an oil change or a marriage certificate ensures a good marriage will Bible reading, fellowshipping with the saints, or giving to the poor knit a heart-to-heart love relationship with our Lord.

Then, how do we build and keep intimacy with our First Love? Here are suggestions from the One who knows: spend time to seek Him (Jer. 29:13), wait to welcome His presence (Ps. 62:1), rejoice in His coming (Ps. 16:11), connect with His Spirit (John 15:5), enter His intimacy (John 17:3, John 17:23), and behold His glory (2 Cor. 3:18). Only then might we confidently speak the words, "Father, I worship you." True worship is all about drawing close enough to Him and He to us (Jas. 4:8) to guarantee an intimate two-way communication about our shared love with Jesus and other matters of the heart.

The number two elevator spoke volumes about avoiding maintenance, didn't it? Like relationships with our car, our spouses, and Jesus Himself, it is a pay-me-now-or-pay-me-later scenario. The latter option might mean a blown engine, a failed marriage, or a major backslide. But, if you expect Kisses from Heaven, then going to Oil Can Harry's every three months, an excessively nice dinner on her fortieth birthday (Did you blow that one also?), and a lonely place for an intimate gathering to worship and fellowship with Jesus early each morning would be among my suggestions.

Am I singing to a listening choir? Hope so.

QUESTION: Where is the Kiss from Heaven in this God Story?

ANSWER: Surviving that bucking bronco number two Midtown Hotel elevator must be the certified Kiss from Heaven awarded in this God Story. Forever hidden within that elevator's out-of-control behavior will be how that car not only suddenly dropped like a rock in a negative-G lethal freefall from the twentieth floor but also, for no reason, abruptly stopped to save my baby girl's life by dumping us off exhausted but grateful on the eighteenth. I have no proof, but another on-call angel's intervention (Heb. 1:14) would have been no surprise to either of us. Maybe a disappointing conclusion to Edgar Allan Poe but to repeat, a miraculous Kiss from Heaven for my little girl and me. Amen.

13

Catharsis in Creswell (1985)

While looking at that holly tree alive with red berries from our dining room window, I knew this could not continue. With our marriage in tatters, to survive emotionally meant finding relief. Although it would be an understatement to say I had fallen short in our twenty-three-year union, considering the next step was, by itself, a risk. Going one's own way to manage this ongoing emotional chaos could spell trouble, and who could predict the outcome? Still, with life coming apart at the seams, there was little choice (if asked today, I would counsel you differently). So, on the spot, I vowed not to care, not to feel anything anymore.

Whoa! What instant relief! In one lightening moment, I had chosen not to feel the pain, and, voilà, a moment later, the pain was gone. How could that be? Answer: That oath had been the silver bullet, and I had slain the blood-sucking vampire within. Quickly putting this fresh freedom to the test, I set about reviewing the hopeless circumstances and heavy burdens plaguing my days. Curiously, I ignored that most recent vow and the Lord's command: "But I say to you, take no oath at all" (Matt. 5:34). Are you aware Jesus ignores nothing?

Living in a dysfunctional marriage, facing an inept Benedict Arnold of a business manager's failure to pay nearly a year's worth of

IRS installments, discovering thousands of dollars of debt incurred by the unauthorized use of an ill-advised power of attorney, many failures to deposit patients' cash payments in the bank, and, recently, being the target of an eleven-million-dollar "bad baby" malpractice suit had been enough to send anyone over the edge. Yet here I was under more stress than ever while cruising this current emotional roller coaster without a care in the world. It did not feel good, but the pain was gone. That would have to do for now.

Losing That Loving Feeling

Not crumpling under that financial and emotional landslide, it had been easy to turn all problems over to the Lord. So here I was one year later with the divorce, subtly acrimonious and polarizing to our family as it was, settled outside of the court system. Then, there were the fifty thousand dollars in IRS payments I had satisfied after my faithful patients had settled their obligations in a burdensome economic era. The medical malpractice lawsuit, full of nonsensical accusations, blustered along until all jurors but one saw through the plaintiff's attorneys' baseless arguments, recognized the cause as a congenital condition (birth defect), and found in my favor. Waking up one morning to a life with no financial or emotional encumbrances equaled a cancer cure. Everything was finally on an even keel; I was a survivor, and the Lord had carried us through. Curiously, I thought it should have felt emotionally better than it did.

    Having had enough downtime to reflect on the last years, only one part of life troubled me. Knitting relationships together in the family, insomuch as others were willing, was so far so good. Financially, there was improvement, which would, without an unforeseen eventuality, keep heading in that direction. Using the local athletic club's exercise facility at the end of each day solved slimming down and buffing up. Then, my new church promised diverse opportunities for ministry, while a recent missionary trip to Nepal had been inspiring. Finally, the

Department of Veterans Affairs Clinic in Eugene, Oregon, of which I was director, was growing at a record rate. Oddly, it was here there came an impasse.

Over the years, medicine had never offered me an intellectual challenge. It would have, had I allowed it as I studied to stay qualified in areas relevant. Working around the logging and wood products industries had demanded extra skills dealing with trauma while delivering babies required currency in obstetrics, neonatology, and pediatrics. Cardiology and internal medicine kept any family doctor with a geriatric population striving academically. Then, there were tropical medicine updates for short-term missions and, finally, having been the sports doctor for the local high school football team for ten years, conferences to stay proficient in that specialty. Honestly, all that "keeping up" offered me little satisfaction; it was simply a necessary part of a sound professional life.

Personally, what made the practice of medicine satisfying was the diversity of patients. Learning what most doctors eventually stumble upon, that there are certain medical conditions generated by the stress of emotionally charged life issues, I headed down this side street. Inadvertently, I found my niche as a Christian doctor, a place to minister the love of God full-time as the ultimate clinical experience. Soon, our office became a city of refuge where wounded people came hungry for medical care and spiritual support. This development put the icing on my professional aspirations while connecting with people in this way gave life added meaning.

As the Department of Veterans Affairs clinic director, a high percentage of our new clinic's population was elderly. At first, I wondered if this older generation would satisfy a need for medical diversity. Always enjoying the large geriatric community that patronized my former small-town practice, here it was no different. Easily bonding with these appreciative veterans, I found their complex medical problems satisfied, if not challenged, my sundry medical interests.

Curiously, it was not long before something was amiss and progressively disquieting. Ferreting out from where this hazy sense was coming at first defied explanation. Could it be the change of location, missing my former patients, or lacking complete autonomy in my work? How about the added responsibility of overseeing and uniting a diversity of medical, mental health, and social work practitioners? Nothing rang a bell, so I remained clueless . . . until one afternoon while I sat questioning one of my most favorite elders.

Figuring It Out

Surveying this gentleman, his morning's breakfast scattered about a long white stubbled beard and then trapped to dry upon the worn overalls camouflaging his impressive paunch, my epiphany came in a flash. At last, here in the flesh stood my dilemma. With my entire attention fixed on this endearing old man enjoying our conversation as if it were the crowning glory of his month, my heart sank. I felt nothing. No love. No compassion. No enjoyment. No satisfaction. Nothing, absolutely nothing. Empty, there was no emotional response.

Reviewing life, without question, my days were turmoil-free—not because I was at peace but because I was numb. Truly, there was no pain. Frighteningly, there was also no joy. Instead, I was emotionally stuck in neutral with no idea of how to shift gears. Picturing myself standing before that window overlooking a holly tree bursting with color and replaying my earlier vow, "I choose not to care or feel," came the epiphany. There it was: the genesis of my present mess. Going my own way denied the Lord His right to walk me through the pain during those last two years. Instead, I numbed up, traded my emotional birthright for a "single meal" (Heb. 12:16), and fell short of God's grace. Move over, Esau! What was there to do? Was there anything to do? Was I to be stuck in neutral for good?

Thinking that way provoked a curious sense, not really a feeling, but as if something from within was trying to break loose; for that, I was strangely grateful but also confused. Searching for biblical examples that could show the way to disable defense mechanisms or medications to discover a breakthrough brought no fruit. Answers were not forthcoming. That left one choice: pray harder (I know—please do not tell the blind man he is blind).

It was a simple prayer, and I prayed it often: "Lord, forgive me for setting my feelings aside by taking that oath, 'I choose not to care.' Please return my emotions." Forgetting to pay attention, sometimes I needed a bland interaction with a gravely ill patient to remind me to petition the Lord again. Days went on to weeks and then to months. Faith available to resolve this issue became borderline; a large part of that foundering state was lacking feelings to reveal it. Gradually, I found myself (more or less) resigned to this emotional lot in life. It was what it was, so I applied a faithless "whatever" to the whole debacle.

An Interstate Encounter

Each day's trip carried us around the eastern edge of Cottage Grove before heading north toward the central part of Eugene. It was a glorious spring morning filled with little sunlit patches of ground fog brightly dotting the budding spring landscape as I approached the Creswell underpass on Interstate 5. Aware that one of my best friends lived in that small town convinced me to call him for an early breakfast the next week.

Rush hour traffic was moving along at its usual sixty-five-mile-per-hour clip when, without warning, I began to weep and then wail uncontrollably. Having no choice, I pulled onto the freeway shoulder, blinded by tears. Remarkably, during this process, my mind was carrying on a conversation with itself, trying to seek an explanation for this bizarre behavior. Feeling nothing yet sobbing out of control, I could not restrain the intense outburst. It was as if I was the star of a silent movie, watching it from above and aware that it lacked feeling instead of sound.

This catharsis continued a full thirty minutes before the tears stopped as instantly as they had begun. Having no clue as to what had happened, I wiped my nose and eyes, took a deep breath, and re-entered traffic. There were no residuals of which I was aware, while everything felt as it had before the bizarre episode. Oh yes, I was a little late for work, which made me unhappy; it was a clue I missed.

What happened during the earlier part of the day at the Creswell exit had slipped my memory by the start of my busy workday. Mornings were an administrative time to hole up in the office to return phone calls, deal with the mothership seventy miles south, a myriad of multidisciplinary clinic issues, and clear my desk of its ever-present stack of medically related paperwork. Today's clinic schedule began at 1:00 p.m., and I would be punctual. Charging through the exam room's door in a "Krameresque" kind of way (a behavior I had picked up from our family GP years ago) while pulling up a small exam stool on wheels, I sat down face-to-face with a gnarled-up old guy smiling over a toothless set of gums and sprinkled with more of those undeniable signs of breakfast.

Suddenly, welling up within were these incredible feelings of love and compassion that caused my eyes to brim with tears of empathy and joy not experienced for years and which I did not in the least try to restrain. The catharsis in the Toyota this morning now made absolute sense; by it, the Lord had forgiven and set aside that onerous oath, opened my emotional prison door, and set this captive doctor free. Praise Jesus, I could feel again. My first inclination was to hug that old guy across from me. So, I did.

Postscript

In a perfect world, people glean beliefs from experiences, react emotionally to those beliefs, and then watch those beliefs and emotions shape their responses. Uplifting experiences give inspiring thoughts, which illicit positive emotions, engendering constructive behavior, while degrading experiences produce negative thoughts, promote hurtful emotions, and result in undesirable conduct. It is not rocket science. Beliefs and their linked emotions arising from present-day traumatic experiences are often magnified by earlier identical beliefs and linked emotions originating in similar (in nature) traumatic childhood memories triggered into the present day. Those triggered beliefs and linked emotions originating from past misinterpretations (lies) of traumatic childhood experiences flood the present and cause mature adults to manifest childish reactions to adult circumstances.

A plain vanilla example would be a four-year-old little girl blaming herself for her father's leaving the family because of her misconceived belief she was not "good enough," which produced feelings of worthlessness. Years later, the father admitted to having become a meth addict as the reason for his abandonment. But the damage was already done because long ago the little girl believed and felt herself not good enough. Have you noticed when facing difficult times, you occasionally react childishly rather than responding thoughtfully as a mature adult? If so, you are more than likely to be embarrassed or ashamed while later questioning yourself: "Why did I overreact in such an infantile way?" Here is an answer: Your still-wounded, unhealed inner child took control when a present-day traumatic event triggered painful emotions from a "similar" childhood traumatic experience into the present day. Then, our four-year-old little girl was crushed beyond reason when her prom date did not show up without calling when she was sixteen. Her date's mother had died suddenly that evening, and there was no opportunity for him to communicate among the chaos. But the damage was already done because long ago she believed and felt herself not good enough.

How does she manage the triggered childhood-lie-based emotional pain for not being good enough when it arises to magnify similar present-day adult distress? Often by using simple defense mechanisms (anger and its associates to build walls), displacement (kicking the dog), projection (blaming others), rationalizing, avoiding, and excusing. Then, if not enough and the pain increases, she may numb herself by formal denial, suppression (consciously) as I did when looking at that holly tree, repression (subconsciously) or, if severe, dissociation (unconsciously). The four-year-old little girl believed she was not good enough for her husband, blamed herself, was filled with self-directed anger, and fell into a deep depression after he left when she was twenty-eight. The husband came out of the closet as a homosexual shortly thereafter. But the damage was already done because long ago she believed and felt herself not good enough.

Soon, simple defensive measures were not enough. She needed to numb herself. The choices were many: addictions to substances, promiscuity, pornography, food, shopping, shoplifting, movies, or other more radical behaviors, which, although briefly diverting pain, compounded it by adding more pain arising from the consequence of using those pain-killing behaviors themselves. The four-year-old little girl's real estate agency fired her for being unproductive and sleeping with a client to make a sale while on speed to keep herself from an endogenous depression and hating herself when she was thirty-three. But the damage was already done because long ago she believed and felt herself not good enough.

We also may use socially acceptable means to manage our pain, such as materialism, money, power, position, fame, education, work-performance-based spirituality, or sports excellence to mitigate it. Even these admirable attempts in excess may add pain by excluding or limiting our attention to essential areas of life like personal growth, social and workplace interaction, or marital and family relationships. The four-year-old little girl went through a successful recovery from substance and sexual addictions and then on to graduate school in law to "make something of herself." Then, when she was thirty-seven, her teenage latchkey daughter fell into drugs and ran away. That produced a backbreaking reactive depression and the need for heavy-duty anti-depressants and anxiolytics in our new lawyer. But the damage was already done because long ago she believed and felt herself not good enough.

Let us summarize: Current traumatic circumstances trigger lie-based beliefs and emotions concealed in memories from perceived "similar" childhood trauma. Those negative childhood emotions are triggered and surface to augment pain already arising from present-day traumatic events. The combined emotional pain demanding relief is further augmented by pain arising from self-defeating defensive measures or even culturally accepted performance-based behavior. The successful long-term management of emotional pain from trauma will never be found in methods to defend us from it but only by uncovering the underlying cause within the childhood memories producing those lie-based beliefs and painful emotions. Then, through ministry by Holy Spirit of truth, we discover the only way to effectively dispel childhood lie-based beliefs (lies) and associated negative emotions is with God's truth. The four-year-old girl could not hold down a job on heavy doses of anti-depressants and anxiolytics, so her law firm denied her a partnership when she was forty-seven. But the damage was already done because she long ago believed and felt herself not good enough. Then she went back to her childhood faith during a second round of recovery, this time from addiction to many prescription drugs treating her psychiatric diagnoses, and entered individual counseling, group therapy, and life skills coaching by the time she turned fifty. But the damage was already done because long ago she believed and felt herself not good enough.

The needed work of inner healing (mind renewal) to reveal and replace our pain-producing lies lodged in traumatic memories with truth is essential, or we will remain emotionally shackled and dangerous to ourselves and others for the rest of our lives. Using trained, Spirit-led professional pastors, Spirit-filled Christian mental health professionals, or inner healing ministers* help bring us to where Holy

Spirit may deliver truth, eliminate pain, and set the captive free (John 8:32). Without me, you can do nothing (John 15:5b) has always been the Lord's take.

During a three-hour session with Emily and me, our little four-year-old girl encountered her Truth-giver, the One who predestined, created, chose, and promised to never leave or forsake her. Holy Spirit paraphrased these truths for her during the meeting: "You are my child (1 John 3:1), holy, blameless and beyond reproach (Col. 1:22), my special treasure (Deut. 7:6), and you are perfect, complete, and lacking in nothing" (Jas. 1:4). Then, there followed a time of personal sweet nothings with Jesus that only the little four-year-old girl could share. Hearing that truth for the first time in her life, it no longer felt true that she was not good enough but, instead, more than enough. Then the fifty-two-year-old woman, prepared by a lifetime of trauma (Rom. 8:26), began to serve as volunteer legal counsel and later an inner healing minister for a non-profit women's recovery center preparing four-year-old traumatized, wounded, and brokenhearted little girls in adult bodies to meet our Holy Spirit of truth to set them free to finally act their ages.

Then again, to be fair and inclusive of other options, our Savior, Jesus, impartial and no respecter of persons as He is, could have as easily delivered a Kiss from Heaven by way of a thirty-minute catharsis on our little girl's way to work during the morning rush on Interstate 5 approaching the Creswell exit ten miles south of Eugene, Oregon.

Instead, oh my, He chose me. Truth is, pilgrim, Jesus is our healer and heals how He wishes, when He wishes, and where He wishes while we, if fortunate, get to ride shotgun, which is always a Kiss from Heaven when blessed to sit at the right hand of Holy Spirit at work.

*Although training in counseling and psychiatry augments Dr. Caleb's fifty-plus-year history as a general medical doctor, neither he nor Emily claim to be licensed counselors, psychologists, or psychiatrists. As Christian pastors and inner healing ministers, we have, however, been formally trained over twenty-five years by several ministries specializing in that latter discipline. Having spent decades ministering in this arena, neither of us would claim to be more than facilitators. Christian ministers eventually learn to lean on Holy Spirit to bring His truth by mind renewal, which only He and He alone can deliver. We are merely privileged disciples of the Master upon whom we depend for direction and to whom we give all credit, honor, and glory for His ministry outcomes.

**The four-year-old girl here is fictitious but often found and universally illustrative of the tragic course so many traumatized ministry recipients have taken before finally meeting their mind-renewing (Rom. 12:2) miracle healing Holy Spirit of truth face-to-face.

QUESTION: Where is the Kiss from Heaven in this God Story?

ANSWER: If you are a believer, it is easy to grasp that God may occasionally use spiritual catharses to cleanse and purify our hearts from unknown sin or pain emanating from hidden places. In this God Story, I unwittingly ignored the Lord to go my own way to suppress pain associated with a life falling apart. I chose to numb myself, and it worked. The unintended consequence arose when the source of pain was eliminated, and I remained numb. Discovering the reason, I repented, sought the Lord, and, when He was ready, received a Kiss from Heaven, cleansing from my sin (that time of emotional numbness, unintended separation from the Lord, and a sad period of backsliding from Jesus), and restoration to a place not only in touch with my emotions again but to reestablish the Lord as an essential part of any patient-doctor relationship. By now, you know who the Great Physician was prescribing the Kiss from Heaven in this God Story.

14

Power of the Tongue (1985/1998)

Most Thursday afternoons during the milder times of year found us (if you include Holy Spirit and Boss Hogg, the white Chihuahua) winding our way south alongside the rambling Row River into the rugged Bohemia Mountains, a range from which that river rushed to form Dorena Reservoir, a shining jewel found south of the southernmost tip of the Willamette Valley in rural Oregon. Do I have you rightly situated? On this day, within twenty minutes of a brief "touch-and-go" at home to load up my Bible, guitar, a pack of cookies, and that jubilant white Chihuahua, our camper-laden Toyota truck, ablaze with Christian praise tunes, soon cut from the main highway onto a steep, unimproved logging road without losing a knot of airspeed.

The music carried me back in time to a balmy Philippine night in a rickety barn where cattle and water buffalo peered disinterestedly from crude stalls as our evangelist offered an altar call to those who wished baptism by the Holy Spirit. A Filipino school teacher, the alcoholic husband of a local church worship leader, had minutes earlier dedicated his life to Jesus. Now, weeping, he shuffled his way forward again over the barn's straw-strewn dirt floor.

Overhead, one bright, bare incandescent bulb swung lazily from a lone wire, its light unsuccessfully reaching the far corners of the barn while wide-open windows invited tropical breezes, heavily scented with bloom, to help freshen the structure's pungent air where light had not penetrated. Seated upon elderly, rough, hand-hewn hardwood benches, those of us attending riveted our eyes upon this new believer standing before the Lord. His adulterous exploits, violent outbursts of rage, and drunken stupors were notorious in the community, allegedly branding him reprobate by all but his godly wife, who for twelve years had refused to let go of Jesus' garment. While our evangelist encouraged all in line to pray for Spirit baptism, two other brand-new-born-again believers wrestled with Heaven for their prayer language.

All at once, the teacher burst into a song without lyrics but a melody so sweet that tears welled up in surrounding eyes, my own too, while invading each astonished heart and to the far reaches of the barn. Never had music moved me, nor had I heard such a heavenly sound come from any human voice. Later, I questioned the evangelist; he said, "That was the Song of the Lord" (Ps. 40:3).

Until that day, I had spoken or sung infrequently in the Spirit because it had seemed to do little for me. That night in the barn, the mesmerizing Song of the Lord held something more profound than music itself. I cannot effectively describe that deep unto deep experience but only that I knew that I knew it was not the teacher singing but Holy Spirit singing through the man. Yet, neither his voice nor the melody moved me so much as the pure spiritual power behind both. I assumed that to be Holy Spirit Himself.

A Step Further

Spiraling up the mountain road, that time-worn Philippine memory continued to ferment awe mixed with confusion within my mind. Then, Holy Spirit spoke, "Pray in your heavenly language." Overcoming reluctance, and for the first time in a while, I stumbled into tongues. We seemed headed nowhere when Spirit asked, "Would you like to understand what you are praying?" Yes, I did.

What followed was unprecedented: A large scroll unrolled in my mind as an inner vision. It was impossible to focus on the parchment because Holy Spirit (by the tongue presumably interpreting the parchment) was using the most unimaginably perfect English ever spoken. That prayer, I knew, was not only truth but a message fit only for the ears of the Most Holy. The vocabulary far exceeded my own and featured unidentifiable words that, for an unknown reason, had meanings I easily understood. It was poetic prose. The sentence structure was precise in rhythm and rhyme. The message was so cogent and succinct that it penetrated my entire being like a thousand velvet arrows, followed by a river of warm oil pouring into my soul. Then, there was an anointing upon the prayer, which radiated the identical power I had felt when the teacher echoed his Song of the Lord months before in that Philippine barn. As quickly as the inner vision of the parchment appeared, it vanished, along with all the spoken words. That experience gave me a deep understanding I lacked for years. No man ever prays unassisted in tongues (John 15:5b). Only Holy Spirit praying through an inadequate man in the heavenly language of angels (1 Cor. 13:1) makes the tongue of a man flawless and fit for the ears of our King. If He lets men in on the interpretation, then praise the Lord. If He does not, then praise the Lord.

An After-Dinner Drink

Emily and I, recently returned from two weeks at the Toronto Blessing (a Canadian revival arising in the mid-nineties), were less retired but more re-fired than ever. Curled up with her Bible behind me in a comfortable glider rocker after supper, I remained studying at the dining room table while silence ruled the room except the occasional rustle of turning pages. Now, my wife never prayed in tongues, although she had been gently contending with Holy Spirit for the gift. Well, that night Holy Spirit ruled in Emily's favor. Suddenly, silence gave way to her voice, booming a message in her newly conferred prayer language.

Startled, I lifted inches off my bench before descending in a resounding thud. Wow, the girl was out of the gate praying in the Spirit for the first time. There was no halting speech or vain repetitions in her prayer language; the flow was expressive and heartfelt as if she had been praying in tongues for years. Excited and happy for her, I had no way to express my joy or get a word in edgewise. And why would I? It was a holy moment.

If not enough, within moments, she prophesied. Emily prophesying? Marvelous! Grabbing Post-it notes and journaling what I could, when her season of prophetic prayer stopped, Emily was ecstatic. Little wonder. She had merely been grazing on the Word when Holy Spirit spoke through her in tongues and then, again, prophetically in English. She recalled neither content from the tongue nor the prophecy.

That night, the Spirit gave me no interpretation for her tongue. However, as I wrote this memoir, I had an epiphany: The interpretation of Emily's first tongue was the prophecy that followed. Of course! So, I dug out those crib notes. What a great Word it was. And what a sweet Kiss from Heaven.

Postscript

If we are true to ourselves (that is a whole different rabbit trail), the conflict over praying in tongues has not only polarized the Church but also taken on a life of its own. There are denominations that believe you cannot have an eternal relationship with Christ without speaking in a heavenly language. That clearly throws down the gauntlet in the face of those who say, "Tongues are no longer in evidence after the early Church and are not for today."

Before we move forward in a more traditional discussion, let us first consider the possibility of changing our thinking, even a paradigm shift, and a fresh way to approach speaking in tongues in the Church. Rather than creatively weaponizing the Word of God, reupholstering worn-out unresolvable arguments, or seeking new ways to defeat an opposing side's view, let us take another road and one less traveled, at least regarding a Christian's prayer language.

We can all agree that speaking in tongues is a gift from Holy Spirit, who alone decides who receives the gift and who doesn't (1 Cor. 12:11). It is also clear that tongues are available when we do not know how to pray by allowing Holy Spirit, who does how to pray, to communicate directly with God on our behalf (i.e., Holy Spirit comes to our rescue as a Helper because we need help).

Doesn't this imply that the remaining Christians, who have not been gifted with tongues, know how to pray as they should and do not need the gift? What logically follows is this: Ungifted Christians praying in their native language are acceptable to the Father and need no help. So, since Holy Spirit is no respecter of people (making Him a fair, impartial, and unprejudicial judge), He merely assigns the gift of tongues to augment and strengthen prayers to make them effective, acceptable, and according to the Father's will for those in need. For those who need no help, there is no need to pray in tongues.

See how this viewpoint annihilates the long-entrenched sense of bias, second-class citizenship, and elitism unfairly projected for years by the ungifted upon the tongue talkers. Shockingly, the tables are now turned, revealing the truth: Those speaking in tongues do not know how to pray as they should, while the ungifted know and do not need help or require the gift of praying in tongues.

Whoa! Let's move forward before that discussion turns into a religious riot. Trying to build an airtight case against the gift of tongues requires us to deny God's Word (1 Cor. 12:7) and, if need be, our indwelling Holy Spirit His right to help us in supernatural communication with the Father. This also blocks Holy Spirit from praying through us when we either do not know how to pray or cannot pray for ourselves (Rom. 8:26–27). One common argument put forth is that we must pray only in a known language, the tongues of men. That slippery slope leads to man binding the Spirit of God (and the Bible) to human will (and known language) instead of surrendering man's free will to the Spirit of grace. That statement alone requires some critical thinking and heavenly prayer by itself.

Resisting, quenching, grieving, insulting, and denying the Spirit are only a handful of biblically stipulated ways to negatively affect Holy Spirit's participation in our lives. When that occurs, we hinder His longing (not His ability) to work within us according to His pleasure. That means not only may He withdraw tongues but His entire array of helps (e.g., comforting, strengthening, standing by, teaching, guiding, advocating, and interceding) plus inhibit the remaining gifts and fruits of the Spirit. Then, we become joints (structure) without marrow (life), religious shells ruled by law (dogma, doctrines, and traditions of men) and void of life-giving undeserved favor of God (grace and mercy).

So, the consequences are severe when we deny the Spirit His right to function as He chooses, when He chooses, and how He chooses in our lives and forces us to become our own gods. Since we kicked God out of our schools, our courts, our government, our morality, and, you could argue, now our prayer life, what has happened? Even more disturbing, "What hasn't happened?" We don't have the time, friend. You respond, "What is the big fuss, anyway? I am a Christian. I believe in God, Jesus, and the Holy Spirit." Jesus responds, "You do well; the demons believe, and tremble" (Jas. 2:19). The scary thing here— who among us is trembling? Not the Lion of Judah sleeping in the back of our sinking boat who, this time when petitioned, may not voice His roaring deliverance, hush the raging maelstrom, or even bother to awaken. Ever think of that? Talk about a time when we will not know how to pray! Or have anyone to help us. Or even time to tremble?

QUESTION: Where is the Kiss from Heaven in this God Story?

ANSWER: The first Kiss from Heaven from this story should be to embrace the incredible privilege we have as temples of God's Holy Spirit (1 Cor. 6:19), our only God on earth who lives within and walks alongside us to see Father's needs satisfied and ours filled, who prays through us according to the will of God when we don't know how to pray (indicating sometimes, we do), and knowing that His prayers through us hit Father's throne room unfiltered, in perfect composition, according to His will, and fit for the ears of a Holy God (Rom. 8:27). Second, He enables us to know Him through an intimate love relationship with the Godhead. Third, enabled by the power of His resurrection, He brings His life through us to the dead in Christ by revival, the lost in our world by awakening, and overcomes the deceit of a defeated enemy by salvation, healing, and deliverance. Fourth, we experience the fellowship of His sufferings by sharing Jesus' pain from the settled rebellion and rejection of Him (and often ourselves) by this world. Fifth, we become conformed to His death by dying to self-promotion, this world's pride and prejudice, and the devil's incessant lying as ongoing preparations for our victorious trip to Heaven (Phil. 3:10). So, Holy Spirit prays through us directly into Heaven's throne room according to Father's will, builds us up on our most holy faith (the assurance that those prayers will move Father's heart in our behalf), while keeping us operating securely in the unconditional love of God, which never fails (Jude 1:20). Oh, how many Kisses from Heaven does Holy Spirit unleash in and through our lives when we merely surrender ourselves to Holy Spirit, letting Him bring His love through us to others, and glory to the King of Kings and the Lord of Lords. Amen.

15

Trashcan Man (1989)

How often since the early 1990s have we passed a sadly indigent soul standing on a busy downtown street corner boldly brandishing a "Will Work for Food" sign while acting as if not responding to it violated an unwritten community standard for social responsibility? The beggar (let us be honest) considered his noble intentions as the only real prerequisites needed to motivate the rest of us to participate in this creative, self-entitled social program. Lucky for him, about everyone understood that the most humane, politically correct, and fastest way to respond to this social dilemma was to keep it simple; just put five dollars in his palm and let the guy buy his own grub. In our busy lives, who has time to shop for a total stranger? At least we could keep a little control and absolve our own (false) sense of guilt for eating three squares a day, even if it meant buying our way out of a ruse.

There was a family enterprise near my office that took pandering to a new level by splitting each day up into shifts among its members. When the authorities, who I guess had little else to do, finally put together a sting operation, that little group of hustlers had been efficiently working as streetcorner entrepreneurs for over three years. During that interval, they had garnished over 300,000 tax-free dollars from the pocketbooks of their unwary "pigeons," which surpassed the annual incomes of 98 percent of their benefactors. How much work for food this family had performed over the years, no one knew. Nor was anyone certain how often others invited these scam artists to dinner or gave them bags of groceries to restock their kitchen cupboards. I feel certain that most marks found it easier to soothe their tender (although suckered) consciences by applying cold hard cash to a (not-so) empty pocket than to bring a smelly homeless person home for dinner with the kids. Tell me, Christian, setting aside your newly offended sensibilities, what was inaccurate with that sad exposure of the sad state of our once-laudable Yankee entrepreneurial spirit?

Breakfast at McDonald's

Not sure that I have yet to learn my lesson around this whole mooching business but, okay, I have not. The first time I fell for this cleverness was on my way to work one deliciously bright spring morning. Braking for a stoplight gave me time to study a nicely dressed (a clue I missed) Hispanic man across the street. You won't accuse me of being a racist by painting him as a person of color with an enterprising spirit, will you? Making him white would have to take him off the street, negate his enterprising spirit, and stand him in line at the local welfare office. We may do that if you choose, but it would put us out of business with this story.

Anyway, there he was, brandishing the first of many "Will Work for Food" signs I was to encounter over the following years. Having ten minutes to spare and seeing him conveniently stationed on the same corner as one of our local McDonald's, I quickly headed to the Golden Arches to appease both this needy man's appetite and my own escalating sense of altruism. "What better way to start the day than by giving to the afflicted or the needy?" I mused.

Pulling across the highway and into Mickey D's parking lot, I dashed in and ordered the finest and most expensive item on the list of breakfast cuisine: scrambled eggs, pancakes, sausage, potatoes, orange juice, and (be careful now) McDonald's hot coffee with cream and sugar. Sack in hand and feeling more than good about myself, I scooted my elderly Isuzu Trooper to our subject's place of business. Stopping curbside opposite him, I reached across the front seat and lowered the passenger side window (I mentioned elderly, did I not?). His expression went from quizzical to outright glee as he approached the car, expecting my gift. In one fluid (and slightly dramatic) motion, I completed my selfless Christian act by thrusting the bulging sack crammed full of steaming breakfast food into his waiting hands. His expression morphed in a flash from joyful gratitude to thunderstruck disdain. "How dare you?" questioned those dark and piercing eyes, "How dare you?" So surprised I had no time to take offense. See, I was a neophyte and yet to understand the profession. Let us just say it was inauguration day for this doctor.

Briefly examining the food-filled sack while mumbling something (not very complimentary, I think) in Spanish, he theatrically released my heartfelt gift from his hand to the pavement as if it were contagion. Then, bravely shaking off this affront and pulling himself together, he at once slipped back into portraying a pitiful, half-starved but well-dressed victim of circumstances, courageously offering his services to any willing rescuer.

He and I had completed our business. We were finito. With a growing line of morning traffic altruists impatiently piling up behind me, I reluctantly drove off. Glancing in the rearview mirror at that McDonald's sac resting on the pavement only made me hungry and consider going around the block to fetch it for myself. (Before my heart attack, I loved those deep-fried potatoes.) Glancing at my watch, I was late for work. Something here, I thought, was not right; nothing about this brief adventure turned sordid calamity seemed redeemable. Oh, didn't I feel a little abused and a whole lot initiated. And hungry—did I mention hungry?

A Rapid Evolution

Since those early days, the pandering profession has risen to a whole new level. Appealing to people for food had its drawbacks; sometimes you unintentionally received . . . well, food. Soon, this flawed guise found itself supplanted by more grandiose and effective ways to twang the heartstrings of the "pigeon" population. Being out of work as a veteran was a fresh idea. Being homeless and unable to work was an even better one. This method soon morphed into "Paralyzed Veteran Unable to Work" signs, which quickly gave way to professionally finished glossies crying Homeless Vietnam War Veteran Unable to Support Wife and Eight Kids" (who, incidentally, had long ago celebrated their twentieth birthdays and were halfway to completing college degrees). This worked well and still does, except for folks like me.

Truthfully, nowadays, I try to rely less on my willing heart than Holy Spirit's wisdom. He keeps me out of trouble. Also, as the physician director of the local Veteran's Administration Clinic, I was all too familiar with those vets who not only received excellent medical, mental health, and other social services from our clinic but were, in addition, often recipients of monthly disability payments (often of no small caliber, I might add) from Uncle Sam (who, my friend, is merely a misnomer for you and me). You might consider me a cynic. How about a realist?

Parting with a Twenty

One dark and previously stormy night, I left the clinic after finally finishing reams of paperwork (a prerequisite for government employment) and thank you, Jesus, for freeing up my weekend. Giddily tripping down the avenue without a care in the world on my way to my trusty Trooper resting eagerly in a nearby parking garage, there he was. Okay, not the Trooper, but this bedraggled, scraggily guy dressed in a long woolen tweed overcoat twenty years overdue for the Salvation Army. Ancient combat boots with heels worn flat and leather cracked by age and capped by a floppy-eared remnant of a Korean War vintage cold-weather helmet liner, he was sorting through a smallish dumpster in the alleyway directly across the street. There was enough light for me to see his face flushed with years of alcohol abuse and his long tobacco-stained fingers with nails proud enough for a *Vogue* cover. He was making no attempt to hide his behavior as he intently deposited a growing number of redeemable aluminum cans into old Wal-Mart sacks tethered to an elderly bicycle lurking in the shadows. Then, Holy Spirit spoke, "Give him twenty dollars."

Okay; now, twenty dollars may not seem like serious money nowadays, but in the early nineties, twenty dollars were worth twenty dollars and bought twenty dollars worth of stuff, while today, the same amount of stuff would cost over forty dollars. Early in our area, ATMs dispensed a maximum of sixty dollars at a whack, a nice dinner cost four bucks, and a gallon of gas went for a dollar plus; okay, you get what I mean. So, right off the bat, my attitude was not highly receptive, mostly because this current event was triggering the still-fresh memory of "old dark and piercing eyes" at McDonald's. Besides, I noted to the Lord, "This guy is clearly an alcoholic." Using the word "drunk" or "wino" always seemed a little out of place, considering I was a caregiver talking to Jesus; besides, I did not want to seem "judgmental" while living in Eugene, Oregon, the politically correct center of the universe. "You know that he will only spend it on booze," I continued.

The Lord continued also, "Go and give that guy twenty dollars." I did not say a thing but reached for my wallet and prepared to head across the street, still murmuring, ventilating, whining, and complaining. This made no sense. The old geezer would just waste this money on "riotous" living, and both of us would be no better for it. Doesn't Jesus read His own stuff?

A Gentle Reprimand

"Look," the Lord began, "what is it to you what this man does with the money I give him?" Now, I was about to contend about who was giving the twenty, but since I often used that argument and always lost soundly, I decided better of it. "If this man's day will seem a bit brighter with a bottle of wine,* what is that to you? Do you know his pain? Do you know his burdens? Do you know his needs? Moreover, do you know his lack of options? Besides, how will he spend the money? Might he enjoy a healthy meal? How about buying new boots? Or share his good fortune with someone with greater lack than his own? You know, I am offering him the same opportunity for blessing as I am offering you. Let us not speak any more about this. I merely want you to give him the money."

By now, I was closing in on the old guy. I did not recognize him, but he was a scrounge, dirtier than a pig, and, in close quarters, stunk like one. He jumped (addicted people do that, you understand) when I disturbed him, now half buried in the dumpster, papers flying high and low as he rummaged through today's virgin trash. His eyes questioned, "What do you want?" Well, to give him this twenty. His eyes now narrowed into a squint, mixing growing suspicion with cautious hope, both of which simultaneously swept across his weathered face. How often had I seen this expression before? Decision-making time! No problem, I knew. Grabbing the money, he quickly tethered his last bag of cans to that elderly bicycle hiding in the nearby shadows and, without a word, disappeared into the darkness of the oncoming night.

Giving to the Poor

"Thank you," said Jesus quietly, as I elaborate what I recall of the one-way conversation that followed: "I wish you could understand what I ask you to do doesn't require deliberation, discussion, or a wrestling match. If I choose to include you in what I am doing, shouldn't that be

Kisses from Heaven, Book Three

enough? How often do we need to go through this in a month? Why do you find it necessary to question the way I do things just because you cannot understand? What I mean (I hate it when He gets biblical) is that you are the pot, and I am the potter. Right? Pots do not talk. Whoever heard of a talking pot? You are to obey, not question me. You are to listen, not to shower Me with your incessant opinions. You are a servant, not a straw boss. Can we just have an understanding? Help Me out, will you? Just do as I ask you to do and learn to trust that my ways of doing things are better than yours, okay? I'm the Ford man here, so I got the better idea." That paragraph is a poor, run-on, wordy paraphrase, but you get the gist.

Don't you love this banter? Jesus is Jewish; did you know that? Have you noticed He always gets the other guy to pay? Have you also noticed that He loves to have spirited interchanges? How often had we had this same conversation? Hard to say! He was having fun with me even as I was having fun with Him. He knows my heart toward those old street guys, and I know His. No difference there. We have spent hours and dollars over the years on everything from alcohol to clothes to food to dog food to Christmas gifts to shelter to travel fares to baptism shorts, to you name it. There have been wonderful times ministering to Jesus the street person, "To the extent that you did it to one of these brothers of Mine, even the least of them, you did it to Me" (Matt. 25:40) and getting to know Him better, "'He pled the cause of the afflicted and the needy; Then it was well. Is not that what it means to know Me?' declares the Lord" (Jer. 22:16)?

Jesus says the poor you will always have with you (John 12:8). Isn't it wonderful to have a Lord who offers us unlimited opportunities to bless Him and to learn to know Him better by walking down the street after work on the way to a parking garage and giving twenty dollars to the first guy working a dumpster? Here is the point: The only difference between loving on the Lord and a "suckering" by "trashcan man" or a pair of "dark and piercing eyes" lies in our heart attitude, doesn't it? Let this sink in, then read this little vignette again. Read it aloud while I'm still around to hear it, would you?

Postscript

Humanitarians are wonderful people, concerned about the less fortunate and willing to do something about it. They put their money where their mouths are. Saying that, let me say this: In my entire life, I have never seen, outside the declared war, which Vietnam never was, more vicious infighting between people, organizations, and nations than I have seen on the mission field. The competition for money, power, and territory reveals not only the system but the human heart running it. A veneer of brotherly love often disguises warfare rooted in desperately bitter struggles for survival.

That makes sense, considering that much disaster relief involves the United Nations, multiple nationalist countries, and powerful charitable institutions. That is a setup for all-out conflict. However, this does not exclude Christian organizations from the fray. They are often right in the middle, only using more of a velvet glove to swing the hammer. I only share my limited experience to illustrate that it is a specific heart attitude issue (not to demean the humanitarian heart in any way) that differentiates true Christian missionaries from their humanitarian brothers and sisters. Let me explain.

While needs to supply clean water, shelter, medical care, food, and rebuilding of infrastructure are common to both Christian and humanitarian organizations, their priorities diverge from that point. Let me be a little redundant. Remember Jesus reminded His disciples that "For the poor you always have with you; but you do not always have Me (John 12:8) and, again, "To the extent that you did it to one of these brothers of Mine, even the least of them, you did it to Me" (Matt. 25:40). Then do not forget, "'He pled the cause of the afflicted and the needy; then it was well. Is that not what it means to know Me?' declares the Lord" (Jer. 22:16). It is good to go over these scriptures again.

Now, well-intentioned people have always pounced on opportunities to serve the ever-present poor. Christians, however, if they understand the hearts of Jesus and the Father, realize that reaching out to the less fortunate goes beyond humanitarian provision to a special opportunity to minister to Jesus. He clarified to the disciples they had limited time to minister to Him, but, when He was gone, they could continue that ministry by blessing the disadvantaged who would always be within reach. That has not changed. We will never run out of ways to bless Jesus the street person and should take every advantage to bless the indigent.

Finally, when we focus our attention and energy on ministering to Jesus, we enter an added opportunity to know the Father more intimately. The gist: Ministering to the poor and needy becomes a way to an even more glorious end by blessing Jesus while including a time of intimacy with the Father. For the folks rescued daily by Alcoholics Anonymous and addiction recovery programs nationwide giving their all to freeing those bound to substances, changing their lives, and making a difference in their worlds, we want to assure you it is a rare event for us to give money to an addict on the street and only when asked by Holy Spirit do we do so. A large part of our giving goes to legitimate organizations with Christ-promoted motives.

However, when the Spirit speaks, no matter the perceived intent, a Christian must obey instantly, joyfully, and completely, trusting Him no matter how it appears or how uncomfortable it feels. Resisting Him and disobeying the privilege to serve Him is a grievous error for any Christian, a short road to shutting down communication with Heaven and forsaking our privileged ears to hear. We must trust in the Lord with all our hearts, lean not on our own understanding, acknowledge him (as Master of everything) in all our ways and let Him direct our paths (Prov. 3:5).

That Proverb may get you a Kiss from Heaven and commonly does, especially when you kiss Him first.

QUESTION: Where is the Kiss from Heaven from this God Story?

ANSWER: In my early days as a born-again Christian, I was consumed with reading and memorizing the Word of God. It was not long until I came across the word obedience in this context: the obedience of faith rather than the sacrifice of works (1 Sam. 15:22) and a word speaking to and penetrating my heart. Responding to His revelation first caused me to long jump my way over that pesky reminder to avoid my life's most challenging feat. Do not conclude that I was habitually rebellious or disobedient. No. Rather, I struggled to obey. It was difficult for my flesh to receive commands, requests, suggestions, and even innuendos without struggling against the pricks.

My intended heartfelt responses to orders often became white-knuckled reactions. Those reactions were based on my brokenness and defense of a false identity (a solitary, abused, and unwanted object). Over time, Holy Spirit-led ministry set this captive son free by knowing the truth while turning the word obedience into the sweetest sound I know. Obedience is a prophetic word and a privilege that guarantees a Kiss from Heaven to a God-given command. God is a rewarder of those who seek (to obey) Him (Heb11:6). Moving forth, Jesus says, "If you love me, you will keep (obey) my commandments" (John 14:15). Notice He does not say that keeping His commandments is proof that we love Him. No. Loving Him becomes a river that leads to desiring obedience of His commandments to please Him by loving others. Striving to keep commandments by human effort (humanitarian works) apart from Him bears no fruit and amounts to nothing in Heaven (John 15:5b). Only Holy Spirit initiated, empowered, and finished works through us are acknowledged as acceptable before the throne of grace. Again, obeying His commands will always be an illustration of His love flowing through us to the afflicted and needy (a very broad and inclusive number of humanity) to please Him. Insomuch as you have done it unto the least of these my brethren, you have done it to me is the ultimate purpose for Christians (Matt. 25:40). We cannot love Him without Him being the initiator of that love. We love because He first loved us (1 John 4:19).

So, to simply plead the needs of the afflicted and needy is to know and please Jesus intimately (Jer. 22:16). Is it not essential to understand that ministry to the afflicted and needy is a primary way to fulfill our God-given destinies in the kingdom of Heaven where only Father gets the glory? Can we understand why Jesus was so insistent on my entering into His love for that trashcan man? Was He also trying to steal a little love from me for Himself that He might bless me in return with a Kiss from Heaven? Why not? Can we see how loving obedience to His wishes is the lynchpin to so many ways to love others, please Him, glorify the Father, and prompt a kiss from above?

♥ 16

The Romanian Shepherd (1991)

On the German Autobahn, we had to be alert: The absence of any posted speed limits encouraged enormously powerful, sleek, oversized Mercedes Benz sedans to rocket by us like black meteors at speeds exceeding 140 mph. That reduced our heavily loaded Volkswagen bus, struggling along at one-third that pace while towing a large trailer crammed with used medical equipment bound from Sweden to Romania, to little more than a bullseye on wheels. At least, it felt that way to those of us huddled inside. Only the twisted metal carcasses of slower-moving vehicles foolishly camped in the passing lane would remain after being rear-ended by one of those German luxury cars, which rarely fared well either.

Coming upon too many gruesome accidents prompted us to set up basic rules of the road. Passing the car ahead required us to constantly search the highway behind to check for any rapidly approaching vehicles. During the day, we held our position on the right side of the highway until an oncoming vehicle jetted by; only then were we allowed to pass. At night, when judging distance was impossible, passing with any lights at all visible in the rearview mirror risked collisions with closure rates up to 100 miles per hour. So, we rarely strayed from the right lane after sunset. Driving the Autobahn was a unique, even challenging, experience for any American driver. For not just a handful, it had been their last. To the Germans, it was simply life in the fast lane.

It was January 17, 1991, and our English-speaking radio station was busily reporting the blow-by-blow beginnings of the first Gulf War. Aircraft attacks on Bagdad had announced Operation Desert Storm to the world as the United States, with its allies, looked to free Kuwait from Saddam Hussein's grip. Ironically, here we were but miles from the action, mindlessly motoring our way through the neat-as-a-pin German countryside. One had to admire a culture that could maintain those elegantly manicured rectangular fields outlined by stone fences in perfect repair and straight as a die after centuries of their own wars. The rubble that had been Germany at World War II's end was a memory. Rather, each village we passed fairly sparkled with neatness and order. We even caught women sweeping the streets in front of their homes. The Germans had historically been a resilient culture; I pondered if the Iraqis were ready to be.

Introducing Romania

Unaware, we slipped into Austria, Germany's equally compulsive cousin. Then, in all her color, came Hungary, a stark contrast to our destination of the newly liberated state of Romania. The trip from Stockholm to the hill country of this former communist bloc nation and Soviet Union satellite had been a long one. Coming upon abandoned Romanian cooperatives, sites where countless locals had labored daily to grow grain and vegetables and raise farm animals for the community, were no more than hollowed-out silent curiosities. Each commune rolling by was a cluster of dirty, whitewashed buildings, barns, and living quarters ransacked by the newly freed and exuberant Romanians, who saw their behavior as a minor measure of revenge for decades of totalitarian forced labor. Walls of the ghostlike abandoned buildings emblazoned with graffiti had nothing good to say about Romania's former masters. For our driver, George, a Romanian expatriate expelled from the country years before as an enemy of the state, it was small payback. Despite the graffiti's lack of Christian virtue, our brother was enjoying its messages with hearty abandon. Who could fault him?

The contrast between this land and the recently unified German Republic or nearby Western Bloc nations was dramatic. Romania was frozen in time by a clock rolled back over fifty years. The ancient two-lane ribbon of ice-mottled highway, which George was gingerly piloting, mimicked our rural roads during the depression years of the 1930s. For hours, that pothole-pocked, serpentine road had led us from the summit of one desolate wind-torn hill to another in engine-testing ascents and descents through forlorn valleys before struggling to altitude again.

We were on a rollercoaster to hell, a perilously paved cattle path that lacked any centerline markers, fog lines, or guard rails. When visibility became severely impaired by frequent howling snowstorms trying to bury any semblance of road ahead, everything else melted into a cacophony of gray. Dirty gray snow-covered terrain morphed into gray hilltops hugged by tenacious gray clouds shrouded by a gray sky. No roadside signs or billboards along the route broke the gray sameness. Only sparsely scattered wind-twisted trees, boasting a handful of dry leaves abandoned by autumn's hurried departure, broke the monotony of this landscape. Next to its vibrant neighbors, Romania felt cold and lifeless, forsaken by God and man, its vitality leeched by years of tyrannical abuse.

Here's Waldo

A gusty north wind, relentlessly challenging our minibus, required our driver to repeatedly downshift the already overtaxed Volkswagen into even lower gears to crest yet another gray summit. It was somewhere during that struggle we came upon a scene, foreign to all but the most elderly Americans. Twenty short feet from the shoulder of our road in a barren field defined by neither guardrails nor fences hovered a solitary shaggy human form, all but obscured by countless layers of sheepskins draped over a body locked in struggle with a swirling blizzard. Only a tall crook held in one hand and a small lamb nestled in his other arm could differentiate this amorphous figure from a large roadside bush or small stack of aging hay. Nearly lost in the camouflage of the snowstorm's gray low-lying clouds and whirling snow were hundreds of sheep blended in a big woolly, gray orb, indistinguishable from their drab surroundings only by seamlessly pressing in about their benefactor and one another. A slew of mental images, much clearer than my eyes were reporting, flooded my mind, all reminiscent of Jesus's sheep-laden biblical parables.

Stupid Is as Stupid Does

Sheep are unquestionably stupid. Ignorance, as I understand, is not having knowledge. Stupid is the inability to learn from it. Four-hundred-fifty sheep followed their leader, trying to jump forty-five feet of chasm; even an Olympic long jump champion sheep would have failed that feat. Are you surprised to discover that all who imitated her bravado never had another opportunity? Then there was the ewe who remained serenely standing in a pasture unmoved while flood waters rapidly rose to submerge her. Frequent are the stories of thwarted escapes when sheep repeatedly ran into narrow slits separating boards in wooden fences far too narrow for them to transit. Tales of sheep paralyzed in the face of danger, becoming lost in barns without their leader, and dying of thirst within feet of fresh water are added bizarre sheep stories. Are sheep stupid? "Stupid is as stupid does," proclaimed one famous American hero of late. If that is true, then sheep give us substantial reason to portray them as so. Where, you ask, are we going with this wandering tale?

A Living Covenant

Studying that Bible-like Romanian shepherd and his all-but-invisible flock amid that blinding blizzard, I wondered if I was not seeing our Master's template for any solid Christian relationship between a leader and his charges. If this template were universal with a true shepherd in the lead, would the four-hundred-fifty have lost their lives to that chasm, or would that solitary sheep have been forsaken to a rising river? Had those other unfortunate sheep been clustered around a shepherd, would enclosures have been necessary, fear of danger arisen, or any died of thirst only steps from lifesaving water?

Wasn't this a living covenant between sheep and shepherd I was enjoying? Didn't it offer a universal solution for the well-being of any sheep? During times of duress, as shown by today's inclement weather, each sheep's inclination was to draw near the shepherd and, by so doing, press into the rest of the flock. Wasn't proximity the surest way to guarantee provision and protection? If true, the shepherd would have unhindered access to nurture and offer safety to his sheep. The desolation around this devoted man was enough evidence he was going nowhere but was committed to becoming the sheep's sole resource and unencumbered by any activity outside their behalf.

At first, the obligations of this covenant seemed to weigh most heavily on the shepherd. He was the sheep's solitary provider and protector. Yet was that assumption valid? Closer scrutiny revealed a measure of symbiosis. As the sheep relied on the shepherd, so the shepherd clothed in the skins of his former charges (sheep killed by predators, those who wandered off, others dead from disease or age, or the blind, halt, or lame unable to stay up with the flock) were endless reminders that despite his guidance, provision, and protection, some of his charges, meeting with unintended tragedy, were guaranteed sacrifices to the predations of life. That would trouble him deeply with a sense of failure and despair. Despite their absence, those dearly departed sheep would not be separated from their master by mere tragedy or death. Nor would these sheep be without an ongoing purpose but draped about their master's body, becoming a memorial to mutual dependence, warming not only his body but now his memories. Even in death, the sheep contributed heavily to the balance of their covenant. How would I remember this picture of a Romanian shepherd and his sheep? The way our Shepherd meant for us to understand His covenant with His Church and the effortless way He designed His Master plan for us to live our lives within it.

Postscript

Considering the sheep roaming the fenced fields in my former home state of Oregon, weren't they always on their own, solitary, without a shepherd, and relying on mere strands of barbed wire to give them security. Was it a surprise to find the remains of newborn lambs or young sheep lying dismembered in emerald Oregon pastures each spring morning, victims of coyotes, cougars, or bobcats? How separated, defenseless, and fearfully alone the rest of the flock then appeared, scattered about the broad limits of their pasture. And how wasted were the lives of those sacrificial lambs in contrast to their Romanian counterparts, where we could at least see purpose. Those Oregon sheep were not stupid. They simply had no shepherd to care for them and, like us, when we are out of mutually devoted relationships, close community with God and each other, are no longer secure from the perils of life.

When we lack covenant relationships, when there is no help in times of trouble, how can we survive? Denied the proper nurture or safety, we cannot but meaninglessly fall to those unexpected hazards. We humans, like those sheep, often stumble into life-ending chasms, drown in metaphorical flash floods of circumstance, fall prey to unrealized dangers, become lost in familiar places, and die thirsting when the water of life is at our lips. At those times, others often judge us as "stupid" for making mistakes or poor choices that lead to tragic ends. Yet we are rarely stupid; rather, we are just sadly out of our intended element, lacking a covenant, and without a Helper in time of need.

Like the sheep, we are never meant to be alone, fenced out of covenant without a shepherd or one another by laws, sin, traditions of men, legalistic interpretations of Scripture, manufactured rules, religious doctrine, or dogma. And let us not forget denominational organizations, cults, politically correct philosophies, wicked ideologies, intrusive governments, or personal walls of offense, unforgiveness, jealousy, judgment, anger, bitterness, resentment, hatred, rage, or vengeance that leave us separated, vulnerable, neglected, and unprotected. Then, as prey, aren't we isolated and inevitably sentenced to collateral damage from lives lived outside covenant.

Instead, we were designed for fulfilling relationships, lives of mutually interdependent symbiosis, pressing ourselves together around our Shepherd who, having sacrificed His life for us as an offering, hopes we will do the same for Him. Extending us an opportunity to be forever one with Him, the moment we cast our lives sacrificially on His shoulders, we are saved to Him and to one another. Wonderfully, as mysterious byproducts of this process, we find ourselves more intimately involved in each other's lives than ever. The closer we draw to Him, the closer we draw to one another. Between people everywhere that is not only called unity (John 17:23), the Lord's overarching solution to all of life's impoverishment and confrontational ills, but even more so the fulfillment of the ultimate cry from our Father God's heart... and truly an authentic Kiss from Heaven.

QUESTION: Where is the Kiss from Heaven from this God Story?

ANSWER: What a stark contrast between Oregon sheep and their Romanian brothers and sisters. A similar condition exists between American Christians and those worldwide. How's that? If there is a word foreign to universal American Christianity, it is unity, which Jesus describes as oneness with God and one another and translates more accurately to perfected as a (military) unit (John 17:21). Recently, we have seen a grassroots revival in Southeast Missouri by the same name. It may be the first significant move of unity among the North American Church since the 1990s Pensacola Outpouring and Toronto Blessing, which became beacons of unity among worldwide faiths and denominations for the first time in decades. It is so easy to see why Jesus loves His unified bride.

Oregon sheep have shown no unity for years and suffered for the lack. Romanian sheep have known nothing less. Not being packed around their shepherd and one another in a big gray orb when the predations of life (or, to be honest, the rewards) seems unthinkable to Romanian sheep (if we can accept the sheep as "thinkers"). Now, there may be a solution to bring churches together as the Church. It may not presently sit well with all pastors and leaders, but when sirens announce the final war or the seventh shofar trumpet the coming of Jesus, the Lord will find His body as one, unified, ready, and tighter than a tic while awaiting His arrival.

Hooked Up by Heaven (1997)

Our Eugene Department of Veteran Affairs Clinic had grown exponentially during the previous five years; now, we needed to add space, but even more so, a full-time lab technician, a position long shared by our already overextended nurses. Then, by a stroke of mercy, here came Emily for an interview, which went without a hitch. She was single for five years, into her forties, had two grown children, and was fresh from training in laboratory work. She seemed bright, motivated, energetic, and willing. What a breath of fresh air! That was enough for me. Hired!

Right away, bringing Emily on board paid dividends. Her easy-going personality endeared her to both clinical and administrative workers. That may sound routine, but to our team, it became more like remarkable. In the medical community, front-office (administrative) employees and back-office folks (clinicians) interact a little like oil and water due to not only dissimilar priorities required by their specialties but the diverse personality traits attracting them to their respective jobs. Makes sense, but not always smooth sailing.

At once, Emily became a self-effacing peacemaker and then a helpful facilitator. She was always early for work, industrious (the root meaning of her name), and invariably able to complete her chores only to go on to voluntarily multitask (a word loved by administrators but not so much by worker bees) by helping others outside her own sphere of responsibility. Soon, our geriatric population, often forgetful and struggling to find transportation to the clinic, were no longer missing their lab appointments. They flocked to Emily, often bringing her trinkets and treasuring the time she gave them to talk. Then, she would carve out extra minutes when her patients needed a little more attention. All our lab problems and front-office back-office tensions simply melted away.

Everyone raved about our new addition. She was a team player and showed that trait both in her daily work and in our weekly staff meetings, where she helped mellow those ever-simmering multidisciplinary waters among our strong-willed professionals with a quick wit, inoffensive humor, and goodwill. Wasn't I beyond grateful? She was a gem, a diamond in the rough; with a heightened sense of ownership, we all agreed that, in the rough or not, she was our diamond.

Considering Emily

Sitting in my office following an infrequent lunch, feet propped comfortably on the desk, hands behind my head, partially reclined in my office chair in a semi-snooze while awaiting my first afternoon patient, I heard the Lord: "Have you considered my servant Emily?" Nearly overturning the chair, it took a nifty athletic move on my part to recover from that heavenly ambush. Also, it was hardly necessary to reply to that rhetorical question. Jesus knew I had finished a house up the McKenzie River, had a fine canine companion in Daisy the dog, and loved my work. The few women with whom I had spent time were skeptical of relationships. (In that regard, I had been of little help.) The Lord knew as well that, after ten years of living alone, I had recently made a selfish, semi-subconscious decision not to remarry.

This is an aside; being familiar with the Lord's ways and having learned not to shine Holy Spirit off, it seemed time to go along to get along. Good things always seemed to happen. So, to avoid creating an issue with Heaven, on the spot, I chose, as the Lord asked, to "consider Emily" as a lifelong partner.

In the 1990s world, it was easier to get by with "considering a woman" as an innocent but unrecognized subconscious chauvinistic attitude in a man than it would be today. So, without giving it a thought, most men did. By today's standards, my "considering Emily" would be judged not only chauvinistic but "politically incorrect," so now I must also plead unfamiliarity with that latter (now hackneyed) expression in the mid-nineties let alone the yet-introduced but now battle-tested noun misogynist, that I assume you ladies may "consider this man" as we speak. I would contend that the use of "consider Emily" by the Lord unlikely meant to consider her as a bondservant but a woman of God. Admittedly, I was ill-prepared to do either. Aren't we glad to have all that stuff aired out of the present equation and upcoming narrative?

Getting to Know You

Having heard the Lord and deciding, after Emily had been two years our employee, to get to know her personally, I covertly joined the folks on Friday nights after work when Emily would tag along. She was so easy-going with people and loved to laugh, did not consume alcohol, nor seemed to have a "roving eye." Spending a little more time dropping into the lab during the week to enjoy her professional but caring interaction with her patients, after a full year of "considering Emily," I asked her to supper.

Okay, I need to clarify this: It was not a crime for a leader to fraternize with an employee, but our organization "noticed" it. So, Emily and I chose to be discreet. On an off night, we chose to dine at the Valley River Inn on the scenic banks of the Willamette River in downtown Eugene. Both of us were dressed to the teeth until Daisy the dog, in her enthusiasm, used one sabretooth toenail to skewer Emily's pantyhose on the way to lacerating the skin over her quadriceps. A small compression dressing later, we were tucked securely into an intimate booth with a wonderful view of the river and each other.

Small talk ensued until, within bland minutes, Emily gently interrupted the conversation and "cut to the chase." (To be fair, Emily says it was humor to loosen up our chit-chat.) "Why don't we skip all this talking and get married?" she nonchalantly remarked.

"UUUUUUH!!!" That was *you know who* unable to catch his breath, let alone answer that question. Had I just inadvertently grabbed opposing clamps of a jumper cable because that is exactly how that moment felt! High-voltage terror raced from one end of my body to the other and back again, looking for a way out. Unable to move, catatonic and pressed into the seat cushion by this alien force denying me escape, my heart was sprinting, my mouth filling up with cotton balls, my mind going eerily senior, and all the while desperately needing the restroom for many reasons. It was a fight-or-flight reaction, if not a full-fledged panic attack. Then there was Emily, serious as a heart attack, leaning forward with her beautiful smile, awaiting an answer. No kidding, she wanted an answer. Well, she would have to wait for an answer because I did not have an answer. One must breathe to give an answer, and I could not breathe. What I wanted right then was... well... a mommy, but what I still desperately needed was that restroom for the same multitude of reasons.

Dry heaves, an immediate bladder emptying, a jolt of diarrhea, a short course of hyperventilation, and one hundred jumping jacks (okay, that's a lot of hyperbole to make a point), and I was back to our table. Oh, that table seemed soooo much smaller, and Emily and I seemed soooo much closer.

By then, the meal had arrived, and the evening moved quietly forward as if nothing "substantial" had passed our lips. But it had, and I, brain-dead as one could be, still heard it loud and clear. With Emily's forthrightness, it was as if the Lord had said, "Decide here and now to not pursue this friendship to relationship unless you are willing to commit to it; you will not treat this daughter of mine lightly. She has opened her heart; respect her for that."

Heading home that night, I was in a state of mass confusion. Marriage was as scary a word you could find in the English language; it triggered so much stuff. Yet here had been this kind and gentle woman being open, honest, and transparent to a fault. If I pursued her, it would have to be with integrity and selfless motive. If it did not work, I would have to face the Lord. If it worked, Emily and I would spend the rest of our lives together.

That caused me an involuntary cold shiver. Did you feel it?

Making the Leap

Two years later, Emily and I were on our way to Reno. It was not long before the appreciation and fondness I had for Emily deepened to love. It was not like the past; it was not all about looks and doing stuff and friends and touching. It was simpler than that; I did not want to face time without her. Being together, talking, laughing, and sharing moments was enough. No, thinking about her was enough. There was never any pressure to perform or please or fit into a mold. If I were out of line, she would just walk me through it. She made it so easy for me to apologize because I knew she had first forgiven me. She was happy and settled and was asking for nothing. When I gave her the engagement ring around Christmas time, she put it on her right ring finger. We had to start over with me on my knee asking for her hand in marriage.

Between my military career and working for the Department of Veteran Affairs, I had built twenty years of government service. Emily and I decided while we were in good health to see what the Lord might have for us. If we waited until retirement to marry, we would have to slog our way through an administrative process more involved than the one I was negotiating alone to include Emily in my benefits package. So, we decided to marry in advance to obviate the added time and paperwork. That put us on our way to Reno to perform a quick civil ceremony before a formal church wedding planned for the summer.

Every mile closer to our destination caused me more anguish. Tonight, we will marry. Oh, Jesus, am I doing the right thing? With anxiety levels escalating above my already out-of-control heart rate, the pressure continued to mount, so by the time we settled into our Reno hotel, I was on the verge of hyperventilating and needing escape. Emily took this so calmly and said, "If this isn't the right time, maybe we need to wait." Can you believe it? She was dead serious. Have you ever felt panic and shame simultaneously? It is beyond conflicting.

Somehow, I settled down enough to call the Silver Bells Wedding Chapel where, after the attendant cheerfully offered to pick us up and take care of all the details, I explained we wished to be wed in our hotel room instead. Meanwhile, that request could not be filled until 9:00 p.m., and we would need to secure the marriage license on our own.

A Kiss from Heaven

Nine o'clock arrived. Emily, in her brand-new outfit, and I, in my freshly pressed suit, stood waiting for the Silver Bells clerk to knock. Both of us had gone to secular weddings and agreed this was not the way we wished. Unfortunately, tonight's ceremony was prompted by administrative needs designed to simplify the onerous retirement process required by the US government. Our "real wedding," we agreed, would occur this summer in church before family, friends, and co-workers. A knock at the door cut our conversation short. Reaching for the handle, my mind painted a small weasel-like civil servant, bespeckled with thick Coke-bottle lenses, thinning hair, wearing a wrinkled suit, and holding official paperwork wedged in a bulging Nevada State handbook. With this image in mind, I unlocked and flung wide the door.

"Shock and Awe"

That would be an understatement. Wedged in the doorway was a couple also dressed to the teeth; together, they overflowed the entire entryway to the room. He cradled the biggest black Bible ever imagined in his enormous right hand; her Bible and hand were only a tad smaller. In they walked, all six-foot-four, 260 pounds of him and five-foot-eleven inches of her. "Praise Jesus," they joyfully proclaimed in unity, "God bless you both."

We later found that Minnie, arriving in Reno fifty years earlier, was found by an Assembly of God pastor sleeping with her little daughter on the church's doorstep. Years later, Dewayne, a traveling evangelist, came to the church that Pastor Minnie had later planted, only to stay after finding his partner for life.

All my heart could do was praise, "Lord, you are so good. You were not going to let us get away with this, were you? We are going to do this your way the first time, aren't we?" No answer necessary.

Our hearts were bursting with gratitude to the Lord, and with eyes welling with tears, it was difficult to speak. So, Dewayne took charge, stood us before Jesus, Minnie, and that cloud of witnesses in Heaven and began. It has since become a glorious blur, but for an hour during the evening of May 23, 1997, this bigger-than-life anointed couple filled with the Holy Spirit and the joy of the Lord prayed over us in their prayer language, laid on hands, imparted Scripture (including the entirety of 1 Corinthians, Chapter 11) prophesied, heard our vows, served us communion, and then blessed us as newlyweds with godly wisdom and encouragement.

The Lord's presence lingered in our room, leaving Emily and I to savor the peace and confidence of the moment well after the Pastors Faulk left. We omitted the summer wedding but have repeated our vows before the Lord, friends, or family on every fifth anniversary since. We also visited Dewayne and Minnie occasionally over the years. Then Minnie died in the pulpit (with her boots on, one might say) preaching one Sunday morning while Dewayne, after several more years of service and another visit from us, released the church into the capable hands of his adopted daughter.

Postscript

If there has ever been a time when Father knew best and found a way where there was no way, this had been it. The truth was, we were not ready for a wedding officiated by a "weasel" (forgive me, I know that is not nice) or, for heaven's sake, to be tethered together for good in a Reno casino. Then, a Kiss from Heaven arrived to arbitrate total peace in our hearts. Wasn't that anointed couple used as a divine intercept to launch our new life? Didn't the Lord know our hearts' desire at the precise moment there appeared no way on earth to have it? How often in our Christian lives have we found ourselves nearly swept over a personal Niagara Falls of our own making in a leaky inner tube, when in swoops our heavenly search and rescue hero Holy Spirit to intercept us at the eleventh hour, patch the tube, snatch us out of harm's way, and drop us squarely into the merciful hands of God?

In the line at the short-lived Lakeland Revival, we struck up a conversation with the couple behind us. We were four of four thousand people trying to out-duel an afternoon sun by hiding under hats, umbrellas, paper products, and headgear fashioned from T-shirts to underwear. Mopping our brows in near unison with our newfound friends, they mentioned arriving earlier in the day from Hong Kong following a mission in China.

"What organization are you with?" I asked.

"With Randy Clark's," he answered. Turning to Emily, "Isn't that the outfit with which Joel Bender is associated?" Surprised, she answered in the affirmative. We had not seen Joel and Susan for years but had shared past mission trips with them. We loved them and their children dearly, visited when we were anywhere near Baker City, Oregon, and knew that they would have loved these meetings.

The couple with whom we were talking stood dumbfounded. He finally spoke, "We left Joel twelve hours ago in Hong Kong. He is my best friend." Well, weren't we able to "catch up" on Joel's and Susan's lives, their children's, and their ministries and to log their new email address. Come on, Christians, do not give us that "wow, what a coincidence" stuff. What is the possibility of making new friends who had, a mere twenty-four hours earlier, left our old friends half a world away? Excellent if you subscribe to God's network of "divine intercepts." Isn't this entire storybook, if you have not yet noticed, chocked full of them.

So, was it surprising that Pastors Dewayne and Minnie Faulk showed up in our Reno casino hotel room at nine o'clock one May evening to change the course of our lives in a singular way? Or to meet best friends of a close missionary couple who we had not seen for years. Beyond blessed, yes. Surprised, not so much. Why? We were subscribers to God's network of "divine intercepts," which depends on Him to order the steps of righteous others (Ps. 37:23) to cross our own (and our own others). It is never a surprise but always a joy. And doesn't He keep doing that wonderful work again and again? The scripture does say, "Whoever believes in Him will not be disappointed" (Rom. 10:11). No disappointment here, Lord, just gratitude for your Kisses from Heaven.

QUESTION: Where is the Kiss from Heaven from this God Story?

ANSWER: Have you ever done something that you did not want to do but needed to do and then were glad you did? Well, we needed to get hitched. I was not mentally or emotionally ready. Still, we had to get it done or be saddled with more administrative red tape to add Emily to my retirement plan after the summer's planned ceremony. So, I did something that I did not want to do but needed to do and then was glad I did. It took the marriage ceremony to be glad, and I am still glad to this day twenty-seven glad years later. Commitment-phobia is often a real problem for many single folks with or without a dark history of marriage (no finger-pointing here but toward yours truly). Where are we going with this?

Well, when Jesus comes to fetch His bride, He, too, will face hurdles. One will not be commitment-phobia. He won't be ambivalent, seek a way out, or be concerned whether it will work. He won't have second thoughts, nor will He feel mentally or emotionally unprepared. No, His primary hurdle will be to get His Dad to sanction the wedding. And Dad? Well, He seems to have been curiously sitting on His hands for over 2000 years. Trying to move Him has been frustrating. Dad knows that Jesus has been ready, willing, and able for ages. He has a place to live; well, there is still disagreement over who owns that hill in Jerusalem. And the new temple? Well, it's being held up because that red heifer allegedly has one white hair ... somewhere. Then, Dad has concerns about the readiness of His Son's bride. She appears a little less "whiter than snow" and not bothered by it. Her church attendance is inconsistent and falling off a cliff. She seems less interested in His Book than her phone, where His Book seems lodged among some unsavory topics. Here's a tough one: She doesn't seem as interested in having a solid relationship with her Father-in-Law as He does with her. There are also rumors she does not believe in hell and once argued for snuffing out the life of a baby girl in her mother's womb because a woman has more right to her own body than a little baby her own life. Then He had heard His name taken in vain, aware of Christians cohabiting before marriage, and discovered other behaviors that seemed contradictory to His Book. Do you sometimes wonder if Dad wished He had released His Son to retrieve His bride generations ago when at least His rules meant something? Father said that if she kept this up, she would look more like a harlot than a bride. Could that happen? He knew it could. Maybe He was overly concerned, and this was a phase she was going through. Maybe He would give her a while to show up for a few church services or revivals to work on their relationship. Yes, that was a fine idea. He would tell His Son that Dad knew He was ready, but His bride needed some preparation time for an Ester anointing before meeting King Jesus in His quarters.

"Okay, Father, you're the boss and always know the beginning from the end. Why not press on to finish Caleb and Emily's story? Please tell us, where is the Kiss from Heaven here?"

"Back at the Peppermill Casino in Reno, son."

"Well, may we hear it? You remember better than we do."

"No way, lovebugs! If we make public how precious was that Kiss from Heaven and most beautiful of God Stories, my Son might choose to elope."*

*"There is a holy familiarity with God which cannot be too much enjoyed; there is a flippant familiarity with God that cannot be too much abhorred" (Charles Spurgeon). My apologies to both the Lord and my readers if I seemed to overstep Spurgeon's line in the sand here. It felt a fitting way to describe the unmatchable symphony Jesus orchestrated and Kiss from Heaven He choreographed for Emily and me on our special wedding day of May 23, 1997.

18

The Tangible Anointing (1998)

In the Spring of 1998 and after three years, the Brownsville Revival (aka the Pensacola Outpouring) was still going strong. Emily and I had not missed one night in five glorious weeks; to this day, we miss those extraordinary meetings. Admittedly, what we share in this God Story is uncomplicated but a tad difficult for the average Christian to swallow. It was for me. Still is. To lend credence to the incident, understand that two Christian adults were the subjects involved, one who was a local pastor and alleged brother-in-law of a prime dignitary in the revival. Refusing to mention any names to safely preserve another man's reputation while protecting myself from libel or labeled as a prevaricator, certifiable nutcase, hyper-spiritual whacko, or home to a demon has made me hesitant to share this tale over the years. Am I piquing any interest here? The brother-in-law, whom we will call Pastor X, was about to lay his hand on my forehead during a prayer session, which routinely followed each evening's message and altar call. Well, try as he would, and try and try again he did, the pastor could not touch me. Now, this is not a lecture on the finer points of a tangible anointing. If you read the literature, you will find differing interpretations. Entire books have been written on the subject. It will, however, help us to break down its common meaning. The definition of the word anointing is to "smear." Often, you hear the term expanded to "God smeared," self-explanatory but hard to wrap your mind around. So, a tangible anointing is a "God smearing" that is perceptible by the senses, especially by the sense of touch. We will settle on that definition, if only because I am the one writing this exposé. Okay? Clear or not, okay!

Right out of the box, Pastor X was a hearty and likable fellow. We were face-to-face, two feet or less apart, when he moved to place his hand on my forehead. As I mentioned earlier, try as he might, he could not. After repeated attempts, he asked, "Do you feel that?" I did and said so. As his hand approached its intended destination, an invisible cushion, which felt like soft foam rubber, was lodged in the space between his hand and my forehead. As he pressed forward, there came a gradual compression of the unseen "foam rubber" until his hand stopped two inches from its goal. After that, my head, followed by my body, would move backward.

Despite the pastor increasing the pressure, there was no further reduction in the gap between his hand and my head but only movement by my entire body in reverse. There was a real, invisible, and inalterable something between us that we both could feel but neither could see. Sharing my laughter, Pastor X continued to push me backward around a small area we occupied for minutes while folks surrounding us laughed back. Then, visibly fatigued, Pastor X retired to pray for someone who intended to cooperate. Emily and I left Pensacola shortly thereafter to resume our travels. Having recounted this story sparingly over the years and then only with friends trustworthy enough to not seek committal papers, I understand the tale a stretch even to hard-core charismatic revivalists. There is another unsolved part of the puzzle: Was Pastor X touching God smeared on my forehead, or was I experiencing God smeared on his hand? Or both? You answer that one. But please, dear Christian, let us not get into those hypothetical "foam rubber" demons. Deal? Deal!

Postscript

So, what was that about? It would be more palatable for most modern-day Christians to accept scriptural stories about Abraham's burning bush, Moses' serpentine rod, Jacob's wrestling match with an angel, Joseph's dreams, Elijah's chariot, Mary and Holy Spirit, Peter's stator, Phillip's transport to Azotus, or Paul's School of Tyrannus handkerchiefs than to accept testimonies offered by a present-day, warm-blooded, and still-vertical saint who was snatched from the jaws of death by visible angels, heard the audible Word of God in a Missouri motel room, went to the outskirts of Heaven on a heavy hospital work night, and was transported partway to a neighboring village when tardy to his nephew's funeral. That present-day stuff sends the miracles-are-not-for-today crowd over the edge and challenges other mainline churches.

Then, to make matters worse, it levies even more pressure on those folks who claim God's Word as inerrant when we recount all Jesus' miracles and recognize His prophetic pronouncement that we are to do things greater than He ever did. Really? Like routinely healing folks or raising them from the dead? What is greater than that, you ask? Well, how about a tangible anointing shared by a pair of seekers touched in tandem by God at a big-time revival in Pensacola? Raising the dead is one thing: a touch by the palpable presence of Jesus, Christian, takes us into a whole new dimension.*

Okay, only a direct confirmation by the Lord would be a believable way to explain this tale for the skeptical among us. However, I will wager my Bible that Pastor X, these twenty-five plus years later, would happily join me in repeating our shared Kiss from Heaven before you could say Jackie Robinson ... or Johnny Kilpatrick, for that matter.**

*Recently, a dear friend, Pastor David Craig of Life Church in Sikeston, Missouri, shared a time when hands laid on him years before by the noted evangelist, the late Lester Sumrall, left David on the floor cocooned and immobile in four inches of tangible anointing for the better part of a day and ruined for the ordinary for the rest of his life. Thank you, Jesus, for using Pastor David's encounter to finally confirm you as the tangible anointing that Pastor X and I shared twenty-six years ago at the Pensacola Outpouring (Brownsville Revival).

**John Kilpatrick was pastor of the Brownsville Assembly of God and Pensacola Outpouring, a multi-year revival in the Florida panhandle during the mid-to-late 1990s.

QUESTION: Where is the Kiss from Heaven from this God Story?

ANSWER: Holding this story until late in Book Three was a defensive maneuver, plain and simple. Calling me a chicken is better than being labeled a liar, insane, a spiritual whacko, or demonized, any of which I suspected may be next in line. To let you know, I expected and tried to prepare for this moment. Two years ago, I traveled to John Kilpatrick's church in Daphne, Alabama, trying to get a face-to-face with the man to see whether he had heard from my unknown partner in this story at the Pensacola Outpouring in 1998. (After all, you must admit, this story would probably stick with you.) So, I climbed the ladder of security at the church and enlisted its top guy to plead my case for an audience with a busy Pastor John, which was summarily denied. So, was I to face the music alone with no way to explain myself beyond what you have read to date? After what seems to be an exceedingly tall tale, I would be met by the secessionist guys saying, "With all your gray hair and experience, you should have known better; we all know that stuff ended when Paul lost his head in Rome." Then, merely weeks ago, while celebrating Pastor David Craig's wife, Harriet's, birthday, out of the blue came an unsolicited tale of David's monumental day when his entire body was wrapped in four inches of tangible anointing following the laying on of hands by the late Lester Sumrall. This immediately left Pastor X and me in the proverbial dust with little need to fear anything more than being reduced to runners-up in the annals of tangible anointing God Story competition. Then where do we find the Kiss from Heaven in this God Story? Oh, in the absolute crazy wonder of it all! Doesn't our Abba have a fine sense of humor when playing with His kids?

19

The Call (1998)

Emily and I were all but anonymous, sequestered among a herd of larger motor homes in a little RV park a stone's throw from the Brownsville Revival in Pensacola, Florida. Only my son in Oregon may have known where in the world we were enjoying our protracted honeymoon. It was not an intentional disappearance from the rest of our families; it simply worked out that way. After spending a couple of cool, wet winter months along the Gulf Coast near Homosassa Springs, we escaped its unrelenting drizzle by heading north toward the Florida panhandle.

Already veterans of the Toronto Blessing, a Canadian renewal attracting worldwide attention, we agreed that the Pensacola Outpouring would be right down our alley while Brownsville would offer a more attractive climate. Sure enough, we were correct on both counts. By the time we had a month of the revival under our collective belts, both Emily and I were getting unsettled, wondering what the Lord might have for us around the next corner. We strategized that Heaven might enlighten us if we fasted and prayed for a week. Maybe Father would give us a call revealing His will and the direction He wished for our lives.

Were we to go on the field as medical missionaries? Were we to pursue an inner healing ministry? Were we to strengthen family relationships? Were we to settle in Oregon, New York, overseas, or elsewhere? Were we to join the hillbilly singers from Appalachia recruiting us? We were considering diversified choices, which felt more like unified confusion. Regrettably, we had no clue as to how to move forward and were becoming increasingly uneasy about it.

It was pushing midnight after Saturday evening's meeting when we arrived at the local Shoney's restaurant (which claimed to be the busiest franchise of their entire nationwide chain), where the receptionist greeted us not with the familiar request of "Smoking or Non-Smoking?" but instead, "Prayer or Praise?" Seated appropriately in the "prayer section," while listening to the "praise section," we prepared to enjoy our last supper before beginning the seven-day vigil of fasting and prayer.

Settling down to develop a strategy on how to present the Lord with our dilemma, we decided that our ongoing cry during the upcoming week would be, "Father, give us a 'call'!" and that our entire time outside the revival would be spent in focused prayer and Bible study to support this plea.

Entering the sixth day, our fast had gone well. Predictably, we had struggled through the first three days only to find the following three much less troublesome. The end was in sight. We had been careful and disciplined, spending evenings at the revival services to conclude each intense day of prayer, study, and fasting. As agreed, we had faithfully made our signature request all week, "Father, give us a 'call.'" The week had flown by, even if our mealtimes had not.

It was Friday afternoon pushing 4:00 p.m., when I prepared to visit the RV park's post office to collect any mail my son might have sent from Oregon. Setting my Bible aside and donning rain gear, I sloshed through the more-like-Homosassa-than-Pensacola drizzle, avoiding the puddles and pondering which was drearier, the weather or our spirits. We had been six days without food but, more relevant to our stated purpose, six days without one word from Heaven. How about more like not one whisper! Or even a hint! Searching the Spirit, I asked, "What is going on, Lord?" Nothing, it seemed, but silence. But hope sprung eternal; both Emily and I knew that Jesus was an eleventh-hour God.

In the post office, there were people sprawled over the counter. Creating a new puddle on the elderly cracked linoleum beneath my wet boots, at long last, the clerk acknowledged my presence as I asked, "May I have the mail for Space 16, please?"

He turned to find the proper box; "Nothing here," he reported to the wall and clearly detached from me. Out of the clerk's earshot, I growled, "Wonderful! First, a week with no communication with Heaven, and now we can include Earth. How special!"

Turning to leave and pulling the door tight behind me, I heard a muffled, "Wait just a minute, sir, you have a phone message."

How could that be, when we had given no one the phone number to this park? I doubted we even had it. And why should we? We had our new Nokia. Reentering the office, I took a small slip of paper from the clerk's impatiently waving hand. Once again outside, I unfolded and read the message. Printed on one side was "Woodworth," and on the other, "Your father called." Then, I read it again and then again and again.

"This message makes no sense," I told myself. Why? Because both of our dads had passed. Then, more like a thunderbolt than a kiss came our "Kiss from Heaven." Smiling, chuckling, and finally laughing, I picked up the pace, scurried around those growing puddles, and backtracked my way to the rig.

Opening its door, I shared my bizarre little adventure with my sweet wife. Puzzled, as I had been at first, she was also. "It must be for someone else," Emily reasoned, "and placed in our mailbox by mistake."

"Not so sure," I countered, "look, the message has our name printed on the front," pointing to "Woodworth" emblazoned on the face of the note, "and the message on the back." Then I asked, "Would you like to know what I think?"

Emily answered, "Sure."

"Well, it is quite simple but nonetheless amazing," I began. "We have been praying and fasting all week, crying out for Father to give us a call. So, He did. See, it's right here on the paper: 'Your father called.'" Chuckling again when Emily saw how the Lord had so considerately sent us a cryptic but personal note in answer to our repetitive pleas during the entire week, she joined in amazement.

The Father's Love

Oh, the love of the Father, the unfathomable ways of Jesus, and the tender mercies of Holy Spirit. Father understood our hearts, didn't He? He knew that we were seeking His will and direction all week long. He saw our longings to know what He wished for our lives. So, when we had asked for a "call," Jesus thoughtfully gave us one.

Sure, it was not a point-by-point clarification of His will or specific direction for service in the kingdom, as we had asked. Instead, He sent us what we needed—a sweet, reassuring, and calming response that clearly implied: "Dear kids, I just wanted to check in and let you know that I was pleased to hear from you. Let us not be in a hurry and get ahead of ourselves. We have time to wait for that 'call.' Why not just relax and enjoy what I have for you here in Pensacola?" I felt the Lord smiling in my spirit. It gave me peace about the future. It was also uplifting to know that Jesus had a fine sense of humor.

Postscript

When stressed and indecisive, the world says, "Life is uncertain; eat dessert first." Enticing the flesh to take impetuous, indulgent, even sinful ways out of puzzling conundrums we face may offer temporary degrees of relief, but when all is over, we will be certain to gain little else. The devil always promises us the sweet and cushy ways up front but will deliver bitter times and hardships at the end of the day.

There is no free lunch or "eat dessert first" with Jesus. He said, instead, "Be anxious for nothing, but in everything by prayer and supplication with thanksgiving let your requests be made known to God. And the peace of God, which surpasses all comprehension, shall guard your hearts and minds in Christ Jesus" (Phil. 4:6). Heaven has a contrasting approach to the devil's way when we face uncertainty. That would be getting to work on our faces before the Lord and sending our requests with thankful, relentless, and believing hearts for as long as it takes to get a breakthrough.

Whoa, that sounds like demanding work, doesn't it? The beginning part of the process may be onerous, arduous, time-consuming and, as was true for Emily and me, end without the precise answers we are looking for. It will, however, bring us a peace that passes all understanding to guard our hearts and minds while Jesus sets about to resolve our dilemmas and fulfill our unanswered requests in His perfect timing and uniquely tailored to His perfect plan.

When we do not have a clue, Father knows best what we need when we need it and how to deliver it. Sometimes, it takes time, but believe me, even a missed call from the throne room can be a substantial Kiss from Heaven.

QUESTION: Where is the Kiss from Heaven from this God Story?

ANSWER: One thing we recognize about Jesus' ministry was His willingness to grant anyone who approached time to listen. Sometimes, like the woman with the issue of blood (Mark 5:25–34) and Jairus the temple official with the dying daughter (Luke 8:41–56), he juggled two folks' problems simultaneously. Other times, it felt like He struggled with fatigue or patience, as with the Syrophoenician woman (Mark 7:24–30), having to deal with His guys' fear while He took a nap on the stormy Sea of Galilee (Matt. 8:23–27), or trying to help clueless Phillip out by saying, "How long have I been with you, man?" (Jn. 14:8–9). Yet He always responded kindly. (Well, a few pharisees and money changers might have taken issue with that statement.) No situation seemed too small.

Emily and I needed guidance. We were unclear as to what the Lord wished for our lives. So, we fasted and prayed for a week. At the end, He sent us a note; it read, "your father called." Our earthly fathers had passed. Our heavenly Father was very much alive and attentive to our needs. What encouraged us was not only His awareness but the kindness to respond sweetly to put our anxieties to rest, even as Jesus always would. That cryptic little note (and our Kiss from Heaven in this story) raised our spirits and let us enjoy our remaining time at the Brownsville Revival (Pensacola Awakening) as a valuable learning experience before moving on a month later to mind-boggling encounters with Holy Spirit over the next several decades.

20

A Biblical Plague (2005)

It was an unseasonably warm day in late May 2005 when we arrived at the lake property in Central New York expecting to see our new home construction complete. What a disappointment to greet a mere skeleton, a foundation supporting little more than a shell with framed innards clinging with uncertainty to a steeply wooded hillside. Our discouraged young contractor, hampered by untoward winter weather conditions, labor shortages, and inexperience, wanted out. We instead supplied encouragement. Then I donned my work duds, set out to finish our dream home and make the young man a profit.

Within twenty feet of the structure grew twin majestic red oaks, eight decades young, each exceeding three feet in diameter at its trunk and towering fifty feet above Mother Earth. Their enormous interlocking canopies, preparing for the punishing heat of a summer's sun, were already casting cool shadows over their domain below. Often the last of the hardwoods to leaf with spring's advent, those oaks, in response to the premature arrival of this year's warm weather, were in full leaf when we arrived. Yet, something was amiss.

Aloft, an industrious aerial herbivore was hard at work thinning out the trees' lush umbrellas and letting shafts of light pierce a usually impenetrable fortress of new growth. The leaves, ordinarily symmetrical, had become reduced to grotesque distortions shed as a storm of fluttering shards to create an ever-broadening green carpet on the ground below.

On this unusual windless day, approaching silence by the absence of any pleasure boat traffic on the lake, there arose a barely audible grinding noise emanating from the canopies themselves. Our contractor shared that it was the cumulative sound of countless caterpillars at work, their numbers having dramatically multiplied over the previous three days. On each successive day, those increasing shards of falling foliage had paralleled the mounting decibels from that hungry horde above. Today, pointing out the obvious, he noted the loss of substance at the treetops was unprecedented.

The culprit, it appeared, was a species of caterpillar that preferred oak leaves to other hardwoods; only the sugar maples ran a close second. Curious, I entered the adjacent woodlands, astonished to see armies of those insatiable caterpillars decimating much of the remaining canopy sheltering our property. While walking the unimproved road bordering the lakefront that led to our cottage, there was no evidence of any damage. Those behemoth oaks seemed ground zero for the rapidly advancing plague. Forest tent caterpillars had invaded our land and our life. Heading to scour the internet to gather information, I needed a tactical way to confront this assault.

Our Enemy's Scheme Revealed

As a teenager during the decade of the nineteen fifties, there were vast areas of the Northeast experiencing an infestation of eastern tent caterpillars gathering to cocoon in the crotches of multiple thousands of trees. Since these insects sought community, individual property owners could limit the onslaught by systematically destroying the tents with chemicals or fire. Unlike their eastern tent-making cousins, the forest tent caterpillars, our present foe, had a life cycle that was solitary. Egg masses placed by adult moths on twigs and branches the preceding summer would hatch up to three hundred larvae per mass the following spring. Those larvae would then ascend to the canopy above, feeding on new growth for five to six weeks. Afterward, each larva would cocoon individually for two more weeks and undergo a metamorphosis into an adult moth. Completing its life cycle, the moth would emerge to spend the following week laying egg masses on twigs and branches to prepare for a hatch the following spring. Could we intervene?

The Summer of Our Discontent

That summer was a nightmare. While working more time to complete our new home, Emily and I occupied an ancient and porous little cabin (converted from an icehouse built in the early 1900s by my grandfather), a shelter that offered little protection from those hordes of nasty beasties. Entomologists estimate heavy infestations of forest tent caterpillars may approach ten million larvae per acre. As their numbers multiplied upon our property, the foul-smelling frass (excrement) from those caterpillars fell from the tree canopies to cover roofs, porches, picnic tables, and the ground itself. Every surface in sight became a bilious brown. The stench provoked nausea, and any attempt to mop up after these insects for more than a day was futile. Frass even found access to our ancient water system's storage tank, turning our only source of drinking water marine green and requiring us to dismantle and sanitize the entire system. The lake itself posted a coliform count by a medical laboratory of over five times the local health department's acceptable limit.

To make things worse, caterpillars burrowed their way into beds, covered exposed vehicles, and made walking surfaces, including the roadways, treacherously slippery when insects were crushed underfoot. Silk strands, secreted during their descent from higher climes, hung everywhere and clung to everything contacted. The trees, attacked by thousands upon thousands of larvae, found themselves stripped of leaves within weeks. The forest under full assault became as a winter wonderland devoid of snow.

After a month, when the caterpillars cocooned, the entire undersides of each building's elderly clapboards were lined with one-and-one-half-inch silk pouches. Two weeks later, after removing thousands of those cocoons, when darkness settled each evening, our floodlights attracted thousands upon thousands of mature moths. Garbed in a mask and protective clothing, I labored four consecutive nights, three hours per night, moving from floodlight to floodlight, spraying over five giant cans of insecticide per night into the moths, engulfing and often obscuring each light. Thousands died during each session, creating undulating circular masses on the ground eight feet in diameter, an ocean of moths dying beneath each light. For weeks thereafter, the whole area reeked of death.

Finally, the assault ended, and within ten days, the trees, including those majestic oaks, sprouted new leaves; within two more weeks, 70 percent of the foliage had returned to our forest. There was a jubilant, although short-lived, celebration until we discovered that forest tent caterpillar infestations had five- to six-year cycles. That meant that we could expect an identical scenario for the following half-dozen summers. This possibility was unacceptable, more like unthinkable. We needed a plan.

Counterattack

Soliciting neighbors' opinions, we jointly agreed to use a chemical spray, nontoxic to humans, animals, or fish, to kill the larvae during the following year. At next spring's hatch, a nationwide pest control firm would carefully apply a spray so as not to contaminate any water sources. The spray the company used guaranteed instant and dramatic results. Unfortunately, the entire remaining watershed for miles and miles outside our properties would be subject to its second consecutive year of defoliation, with the rolling green hills of summer again replaced with the dry, colorless drab of a counterfeit winter. Although a small comfort, we knew that the green would gradually return to all the trees on the lake within weeks. Still, a proactive stance to spray would save our trees years of stress. Whether other neighbors would follow remained to be seen.

Could the surrounding forest survive this insult year after year? The literature was controversial. The less-hardy trees were even now showing signs of failing. And the spraying? Well, it was expensive and cause for concern as a potential health hazard if not applied carefully and correctly. It was an ongoing ecological conundrum. For this year, we had done what we could for now.

At the Ready, Well-Armed, but Uninformed

We timed our arrival at the lake the following May to precede the expected hatch. The spray company asked us to let them know when the larvae appeared. Cool weather prevailed early in the month but soon enough gave way to warmer days—but no caterpillars. Astonished, over the next weeks, I found no hatches surrounding the homestead. Then, intrigued, I cruised the woods to look elsewhere; the only egg masses were old shells. Over the remaining summer months, there were but two trees where more than one or two caterpillars were feeding; these larvae seemed lethargic and lacked the size of the previous year's hatch. What an enigma. Not until early autumn did a local farmer share in passing a unique and unsolicited story that instantly cleared up the confusion, answered all questions, solved the puzzle, and revealed the reason for the permanent interruption and end of the five-year cycle of our forest tent caterpillar plague.

Hot as Summer, Cold as Winter

Unknown to us, while we were traveling the previous winter, a peculiar and rare weather phenomenon happened at the lake. The average temperature for the area hovers near thirty degrees Fahrenheit for the majority of January. This past year, there inexplicably came a short but rapid onset of warm weather (a January thaw) where the temperature suddenly rose to approach seventy degrees. That's correct; the ambient air reached the high sixties Fahrenheit in January, a remarkable and near-record-setting event in Central New York. It also prompted forest tent caterpillar egg masses to hatch as if it were early June.

Quickly, thousands of tiny tent caterpillar larvae climbed to the highest branches of their trees only to find no edible foliage. So, as should be expected, these larvae began to die of starvation. Then, in one catastrophic moment, the temperature plunged to its near winter normal of thirty degrees. Instantly, thousands upon thousands of silk strands streamed from the treetops as freezing and dying caterpillars plummeted to their deaths. No more confusion. No more conundrum. No more questions. No more biblical plague. No longer a need to spray. Only a magnificent Kiss from Heaven. Now, we understand what set our forest free of that biblical plague; would you like to know why? Of course. Then, sit back, relax, and enjoy the rest of this God Story.

Postscript

Well, here we go. Emily hates bugs. The word "hate" in her case is unquestionably a major understatement; Emily's feelings for those critters redefine and give new meaning to that cruel word. In her worldview, those slimy forest caterpillar beasties received no grace as God's creatures. Rather, Emily saw them as energetic enforcers of an epic plague of biblical proportions and monstrous hordes of hell.

So, as I recall, it was when those caterpillars shared her pillow or ended up squished as she rolled over at night in the previous summer's primitive bed that Emily disappeared into hyper-prayer during the summer of our discontent. Those critters never had a chance because my wife never quit pleading for the Lord to move on her behalf and against those foul interlopers. Earnest prayers rang out in the courts of Heaven day and night from my Emily's prayer closet for months.

Listen to the Lord in these scriptures: "Put Me in remembrance, let us argue our case together; State your cause, that you may be proved right" (Isa. 43:26). How about "now shall not God bring about justice for His elect who cry to Him day and night, and will He delay long over them? I tell you that He will bring about justice for them speedily" (Luke 18:7–8). Pleading, arguing, and crying day and night is not a walk in the park for anyone, and it seemed an eternity before my wife saw Jesus deliver a favorable verdict.

The verdict? A miracle, near-record-setting January temperature spike, an unseasonable hatch, a lightning drop to near freezing, and, voilà, no more bugs. Zero! Zip! A biblical plague nipped in the bud by prayerful assault into the throne room of Heaven. Have you a better opinion, friend? Luck, karma, coincidence? Come on, Christian, not by a God who orders your every step and hears your every prayer. It was a blood, sweat, and tears miracle. It took everything Emily could muster so Jesus could do the rest. We thank you, Sweetheart. And thank you, Lord, for another Kiss from Heaven.

Years before, I had heard Rudy Giuliani, the former mayor of New York and presidential hopeful in 2008 and 2012, vaunting his sole but well-deserved victory before the Supreme Court of the United States. Well done, Rudy, well done! But let us not forget about our Emily winning her life-changing environmental deliberation before the Supreme Court of Heaven. Well done, Emily, well done!

Say, here is a thought: What about Emily for president? Say, that would be another Kiss from Heaven. Not sure I could fill the shoes of a First Gentleman... nor wish it upon you.

QUESTION: Where is the Kiss from Heaven from this God Story?

ANSWER: Oh my, we were facing up to six years of a biblical-like plague of caterpillars. Then Emily went to work in her prayer closet over the next months to find that the Lord had quietly answered her prayers by raising the outside temperature from freezing to a near seventy degrees during the past winter, causing millions of forest tent caterpillar larvae to hatch but soon succumb to another freeze a few days later. What an amazing Kiss from Heaven from our one-of-a-kind Father God. The same from His praying daughter, Emily. Wouldn't you agree?

21

No Stranger to Paradise (2007)

The Philippine Islands are a bona fide tropical paradise. Floral tapestries splashing trees, brilliantly adorning porches, and racing brightly along home security walls bring warmth to the eyes and perfume to the senses. Nothing, however, can challenge the priceless array of beautiful golden-brown Filipino faces that welcome one's arrival with shimmering seas of smiles. How Emily and I would miss this land and our precious treasure trove of newfound friends.

It was 2007, and we were at warp speed to complete six arduous weeks laboring with Holy Spirit to minister inner healing to members of our hosts' thriving church south of Manila. We had met Pastor Noli Cadelina and his wife, Donna, nine years before at the Toronto Blessing, but not until recently had we visited them on their own turf.

Reflecting on those inner healing sessions invariably takes us back to but one, the last session of our last day. The brother-in-law of the church's associate pastor, a man who had traveled hundreds of miles from a distant island to seek prayer, was to be our final ministry recipient preceding our departure to the States. The church's associate pastor, his ten-year-old son in tow, ushered the man through our flower-strewn gate. Then, as a group, we entered our small home to exchange pleasantries before the pastor and his son's departure.

Three hours later, having seen the Lord set another captive free, we called the pastor to pick up his guest. Within minutes, the sound of a car horn echoed over the property's security wall. In haste, the three of us headed toward the gate while the associate pastor and his son were already in a dash to meet us midway across the front lawn.

An Agitated Pastor

Wearing a quizzical, if not baffled, look, the pastor first asked if everything had gone well during our session. We responded that it had, his brother-in-law confirming that opinion with a nod. A fleeting look of relief crossed the pastor's face but not enough to dislodge the puzzled expression that camouflaged his usually placid demeanor. The blazing heat of an unrestrained noonday sun was punishing our faces, and I thought it better to carry any further discussion into the cool recesses of our small but air-conditioned quarters.

Regretfully, I missed that opportunity as the pastor, deeply embedded in his second inquiry, sent a barrage of questions culminating with, "Did you or did you not bring your daughter with you to the Philippines?"

"What a peculiar question?" was my thought. We had been with this man for countless hours over the previous six weeks. Having greeted us at customs, he knew we had arrived unaccompanied to the islands, and yet here he was pressing us for unknown reasons about something he already knew. The tone of his ongoing interrogation gradually felt more like an inquisition. Was he implying that we had smuggled someone into his country? How very strange and unlike the man.

Has anyone ever asked a question you felt demanded more than a "yes" or "no" answer, a time when you felt compelled to amplify, expand, or clarify a reply just because of the phrasing of the question? Well, for me, here came that occasion. It was as if the plain vanilla truth was not enough.

Predictably, I felt pressured to detail answers or risk added scrutiny. Also, understandably, I became a tad defensive and tried to clarify my answer with way too many words: "I have three daughters; they are presently living in Oregon and North Carolina, busy with their families, careers, or education. Emily and I have not seen them in months. I did bring my eldest daughter to the Philippines in the 1980s but not since. Emily and I came alone this time, just the two of us. Why do you ask? Is there something amiss?"

"Well," the pastor continued, now a bulldog tenaciously tugging at a bone, "what about other Americans? Are there any other American women with you?" I felt confused, a little trapped, and a tad more irritated. Without question, the guy had a hidden agenda, and without question, I needed to get ministry around my knee-jerk response to this sudden onslaught.

Under that blazing sun, I was feeling like an over-cooked rotisserie chicken while facing this man on a mission, generating even more heat. Without hesitation, I cut to the chase and fired another volley from the hip, hoping to put the ball back in his court, "Pastor, we are the only Americans here. Our landlady and her family are Filipinos. There have been no other Americans here since our arrival. Why do you ask? Please tell us if there is something wrong."

Again, no immediate response followed; there was, however, a pregnant pause. Imperceptibly at first, the pastor began to visibly relax; then, his agitation and intensity gradually morphed into a broad grin. "Let me tell you what happened earlier today," he offered.

"Now," I thought, "we are getting somewhere. I am certainly open to that course change; thank you, merciful Jesus." Hoping that course change might include us gathering around our little 5000 BTU window air conditioner busily buzzing a lonely tune, but a couple dozen steps away was another disappointment. Are you familiar with this scripture: "Hope deferred makes the heart sick" (Prov. 13:12)? We could add, "Along with the entire body, especially when it's really hot!" if the scripture allowed it.

A Confused Little Boy

"After dropping off my brother-in-law," the associate pastor continued, "my son began to ask of me the identical questions I have of you. I was unable to answer him with certainty because I was unaware of anyone sharing this little compound with you folks. Perplexed with his line of questioning as I see you are with mine, I turned the tables and asked my son the same question you have repeatedly asked of me: 'Why, son, do you ask? Is there something wrong?'"

The pastor said that his little boy had become excited, looked his father straight in the eye and shared his story, "Daddy, I hope you will believe me. Today has been very confusing. I did not understand why everyone went inside the little house this morning without a word. Aren't we, as Christians, to be friendly and hospitable?"

Then pastor confessed that following his son's question, he had become increasingly baffled. "Confused about what, son?"

"Well," the boy continued, "why didn't we take time to meet and welcome the American girl waiting at the front door?"

His father, now struggling to keep up, countered, "What American girl, son?"

"The blonde girl at the doorway, Daddy, the pretty American girl who was dressed in the shiny white dress and smiling so beautifully at us," the boy replied, now clearly bewildered with his father's confusion.

Pastor continued, relating that, while listening to his son, he backtracked through that morning's meeting with no recollection of seeing any stranger, let alone an American girl at our home's doorstep.

Disturbing his father's thought, his son interrupted, "She stood beside the door while you adults entered, bypassing her as if she didn't exist. Following you, I stopped at the entrance to catch her attention; she just stood silent, smiling at me. Concluding that she must be our friend's daughter or another visitor from America, I followed you inside. When we left the house for the church, she was nowhere in sight, though I searched."

By now, the pastor's intensity was winding up again. "I was dumbfounded by my son's questions; I had seen no lovely girl nor anyone else at the doorway. Can you understand why I have been so intent to discover whether there were others who could confirm what my son reported? This boy of mine," the pastor continued, "is a very honest child. With his spontaneity and probing, I have no doubt that what he saw was real. He is also a kind, sensitive, and friendly boy. That he was troubled, puzzled, and disappointed by our lack of hospitality and failure to properly welcome this 'American girl' into the home reinforced my conviction someone was at that doorway." Watching the pastor as he awaited my response, instantly everything became clear to the rest of us.

A Sighting

Our conclusion was unanimous, and our puzzle solved. Filled with wonder and joy but a tad disappointed that the Lord had not opened all our eyes to that angel, it came as no surprise. Still, our being an unwitting part of a heavenly visitation was a joy beyond words. That day, the Lord had orchestrated an angelic encounter exclusively for the eyes of a little ten-year-old boy. He would be the sole witness to have seen past the veil of this world and into another realm. He alone had miraculously seen the truth made manifest, that Heaven sends angelic beings to the Lord's people. He would forever understand that truth with a guarantee based not only on the Word of God but also upon his own experience. What a glorious moment for the boy's father. What greater joy is there for a parent than to know that Jesus is personally and tangibly involved in their child's life? As for Emily and me? This visitation, though once removed from the real-time experience of a beautiful little boy, was the full realization that Jesus, our eleventh-hour God, was also showing us that during our six arduous weeks of ministry, we had not been alone but supported by Heaven's ministers the entire time.

No surprise was it that things had gone so well; we were working hand and hand with angels. Wasn't it a confirming Kiss from Heaven to know that?

Postscript

The Bible mentions days of Heaven on Earth. These are times when the kingdom of Heaven comes, and the will of the Lord is done on earth as it is in Heaven. Is there any other way to understand why heavenly events occasionally occur among us or why we spend moments in heavenly realms? The interface between this world and Heaven is not an oil and water one. Instead, there seem spiritual tides that ebb and flow between the two realms in tune with the Lord's unseen timetable. It may appear on the surface that all we need is to be at the seashore, the interface between worlds, at the right time to catch a tide coming to Earth or going to Heaven. Perhaps. But isn't it more often a moment of surprise when a supernatural event occurs? What a conundrum we have in predicting the workings of God.

Are there ways to increase the potential for catching a tide? Sure, but trying to be at the seashore without a timetable is not one of them. Waiting for His timing and the Spirit's leading are essential. Hungering and thirsting after Him, patiently awaiting Him in silence, and desiring His presence more than anything is primary. Seeking Him in His endeavors rather than plunging ahead into our own is a crucial consideration. Yet a devotion to what Jesus is doing on the earth, while necessary, is never enough. I know that it has more to do with complete surrender and obedience to Holy Spirit in any undertaking than the significance or effort given the work. Humble, sacrificial attitudes and teachable spirits also provoke Heaven's favor.

Willingness for us to deny ourselves, be of service to others, last in line, underappreciated, or even ridiculed, reviled, and persecuted have special meanings to the Lord. Then, suffering for righteousness always penetrates the heart of the Father. Sacrificing for His glory—and not for money, power, influence, fame, prestige, or to make our names known—is a big kahuna to surf His special breakers. Above all criteria, knowing Him intimately will get you the most glorious ride available, the ultimate Kiss from Heaven. Welcoming strangers unawares who are angels ranks high on the list. Our associate pastor's young son confirmed that observation, don't you think?

What remains a mystery is this stuff remains a mystery. But it is fun to hover over, isn't it? As are most Kisses from Heaven. Amen.

QUESTION: Where is the Kiss from Heaven from this God Story?

ANSWER: Truly an angel's unaware story. However, not to one ten-year-old son of a local Filipino pastor who alone met an angel who looked like a beautiful "American girl" clad all in white standing beside the entrance to Emily's and my little home in the Philippines. We were busy mornings and afternoons praying for Pastor Noli Cadelina's flock. Despite some minor language issues, our ministry was highly successful, with over sixty folks being saved, healed, and/or delivered during six weeks. Well, no wonder—we had angelic help. There are several Kisses from Heaven in this God Story, followed sadly by many tears. We shortly lost Pastor Noli as a vibrant and influential young family man and friend with a devotion to seeing Jesus save many in Asia's 10/40 window to a premature stroke (cerebrovascular accident). We miss you, Brother Noli, as do so many, but will see you again soon. Keep a lookout, my friend.

22

The Boat Keys (2008)

The summer of 2008 in Upstate New York was a maverick. The months most often warm and dry had not been, while those usually cool and wet had also been contrarian. Those topsy-turvy climate changes eventually were the heralds of a hurricane season featuring Gustav and Ike and an equally turbulent atmosphere surrounding that autumn's presidential campaign. None of the above deterred our children and grandchildren from making their yearly pilgrimages to our modest home nestled alongside the shimmering waters of Skaneateles Lake, a sixteen-mile-long liquid jewel carved out of limestone by a receding prehistoric glacier but now bordered by old-growth hardwood forests and spring-fed to become the second purest body of water in North America.

For all of her storied past, from submersion beneath ancient seas (confirmed by fossilized coral beds that punctuate her eastern shoreline), being a part of a proud Native American Iroquois nation that roamed her shores, and crowned by early twentieth-century exploits glittering with tales of giant steam-driven paddle wheelers ferrying passengers to world-renown spas and medical clinics using her "healing waters" to treat many illnesses, it has astonishingly enough never been these attributes that have portrayed her as a slice of Americana. Rather, it has always been the sumptuous, verdant rolling hills checkered with fields lush with various crops, dairy farms dotted with salt and pepper Holsteins eager to share their freshest cream, scattered apple orchards, and (of late) vineyards heavy with succulent autumn fruit thriving and tucked among many intimate little villages populated with lifelong neighbors, close-knit relatives, and a sense of community second to none.

Despite all her captivating history and present-day appeal, there lurks beneath the darkest and deepest of her waters a "Nessie" (Loch Ness) wannabe, a frequently sighted leviathan of ethnocentric community protectionism which, when provoked, surfaces to work tirelessly (and even malevolently, if necessary) to preserve the area's squeaky clean and inviting upscale image adequately illustrated, I perceive, by the following vignette.

Summer Visitors to Remember

During the Clinton years, the president and first lady vacationed on the lake's shore at the home of friends. Unfortunately for the first couple, the summer following found even the most longsuffering of the locals less than willing to spend another month enduring the president's frequent pizza cravings—which would drive him willy-nilly (pardon the intended pun), along with hordes of intensely vigilant, if not intrusive, secret service agents into the heart of the village of Skaneateles, which occupies the northern reaches of the lake's shoreline. When taking these frequent unscheduled trips, the president's pizza forays were forcing working citizens to detour from their own chosen destinations, personal homes, workplaces, medical clinics, community centers, restaurants, shopping centers, and other places of necessity.

After negative data proved that the Clintons' frequent, indiscriminate "boarding up" of the town for security reasons had become an economic liability to this small village's reliance on seasonal visitors, the high-profile couple chose not to return the following year. Well, the truth be known, the town encouraged them not to return.

Banished, even impeached, might be a more suitable way of describing the whole sordid affair. Anyway, it took years for the turmoil over that testy time of tempest in a teapot to retire its last holdout, when a specialty sandwich shop in the center of town mercifully removed a unique but less-than-controversial long-term sandwich entrée from its menu, the "Hillary Special-Mostly Baloney." Anyway, that is how one modern-day legend has it.

A Summer Storm

As I mentioned, during the summer of 2008, though unquestionably no fault of the Clintons and admittedly years after their uncharacteristically humbling retreat, the long arm of Hurricane Ike gripped the Skaneateles area. Wind gusts nearing sixty miles per hour swept her village, lake, and surrounding communities, wreaking havoc and adding all her residents to over 100,000 other "Upstaters" who lost electrical power. The grinding winds woke and then sent me scurrying to the beach at 2:00 a.m., where, illuminated by the light of an eerily bright moon shining from a windswept sky, I could see my son's twenty-two feet of runabout bucking giant white crested waves and severely trying its buoy seventy feet off the dock. To make things more complicated, the boat's cover had partially detached and was flailing madly in the blow. Following a touch-and-go battle of thirty minutes, I retrieved and then secured the hapless craft to the leeward side of the dock, refastened the tarp, and, quasi-confident that the boat would remain in place, climbed the forty-six steps (but who is counting at three in the morning) to the cabin above.

Later the following afternoon, with the gale winds subsiding and before mooring the craft in the waters off the dock again, I donned my snorkeling gear to enter the always brisk (less experienced folk say colder than a witch's smile) water to search unsuccessfully for a small fastener lost during the storm that I had fashioned to help batten down the boat cover. Twenty minutes later, with chattering teeth and overt cyanosis, I ascended the stairs to discover that not only was the fastener lost, but our only set of boat keys as well.

Assuming those keys were still in the ignition and seeing the wind again whipping up the lake, I decided that tomorrow would be soon enough to recover them. One wrestling match per day with that monster boat was more than enough for any old, cold, chattering blue guy.

What a gorgeous, calm, pushing eighty degrees sunbaked morning greeted us to celebrate Emily's special day. Coffee over, I kissed the birthday girl and then made a beeline for the beach, intending to make short work of rescuing the keys from the monster boat's ignition. Retrieving it was a much more elementary task in wind-free conditions. Securing the runabout to the dock cleats, I partially freed one side of the now-taut cover and wiggled my way inside the boat's passenger compartment. Moving toward the bow on hands and knees, eyes becoming accustomed to the diminished light, I was astonished to find no keys in the ignition. If the keys were not in the boat, then where? Truthfully? Anywhere!

Forming a Search Party

"Let us take the old pontoon (boat) and cruise the beach to the south," I proposed to Emily, arriving on the scene but looking a little quizzical. "Look," I explained with desperation, "the wind was from the north for the last two days, and if the keys somehow fell into the water, they would have been swept south. They are attached to a chartreuse cylindrical float about three inches in length and an inch in diameter. It should be easy to spot if washed ashore."

Emily agreed as we boarded the pontoon, lashed to the other side of the dock, cast off the lines, and cruised slowly down the shoreline. Moving through the shallows required close attention since our propeller was at risk. Simultaneous scanning the shoreline was no easy task either. True, there were open beaches of fine gravel, but others housed larger rocks, even boulders. Then, we had to avoid countless overhanging limbs flush with large summer leaves that obscured our view. Two hundred yards beyond was a large point of land jutting one hundred or more feet into the lake, which often served as the final resting place for lost articles floating down the lake. Our confidence had ebbed by the time we reached and surveyed that large point without finding our quarry. Disappointed, we came about and headed home.

Since the keys turned up missing, I had repeatedly sought the Lord, as I do more often over the last few years than I care to admit: "Lord, you know exactly where those keys are located, but we certainly do not." The Lord commonly uses Emily to find my missing stuff, but she was busy for the rest of today, leaving me in a pinch. Closing in on the dock, I was impressed in my spirit (an unction of sorts) to survey the same stretch of beach but this time on foot. Lots of luck without Emily's eyes.

The Key to a Kiss from a Missing Key

Trekking south along a calm shoreline, the beach consisted of miniature pieces of limestone gravel, each stone rubbed smooth by years of wave-driven contact with its neighbors. Scanning the area not only for the lost keys, at the same time, I kept my eyes open for "lucky stones" (small pieces of limestone meticulously eroded through and through over time to form small circular holes). Hey, I was looking for all the help I could get, so the journey began. The fine gravel at the water's edge gave way in a comfortably familiar fashion beneath my worn-out New Balance running shoes until that gravel morphed into vertical walls of shale, defining the waterline and forcing me onto a rocky bottom in chilly calf-deep water. About one hundred yards into the forage, alternately avoiding and then pressing through the low-hanging hardwood and hemlock branches paid no dividends. Determined, I pressed on, paying close attention for any signs of color or shape that might distinguish the key float from the green moss-covered rocks now dominating the shore.

Continuing my pleas of, "Lord, you know where those keys are located, and I certainly do not," unexpectedly, this comment came to mind: "You are correct; I do know the location of those keys. Why not ask me to show you where to find them?" Wow, here was an epiphany easily understood: I was not being specific enough with Jesus.

Okay. What I had been repeating for two days was true. He knew where the keys were. And by His intervention, He wished me to know also. If I was interpreting Holy Spirit's communication correctly, I needed to be more to the point. Specifically, what did I want? That was easy. "Lord," I spoke aloud, "you know the location of the keys, and I do not; now, would you show me?"

Whether it was five or ten more steps, I am uncertain. I was still ruminating over my discussion with the Lord while struggling to convince my eyeballs to scan the beach when, you know by now, standing erect between two softball-sized mossy green rocks to gain my attention was a little faded chartreuse float with a shining set of boat keys dangling proudly at its side. Thanking the Lord with a deep sense of gratitude, you might conclude my appreciation was for rescuing those keys. Yet there was so much more. Standing in that calf-deep water, eyes focused on those now-captive keys, my mind slipped back a week to a place where I had been openly, even emotionally transparent with Jesus: "Lord, it has been over a year, and that angel sighting in the Philippines since you have made yourself known with a Kiss from Heaven. I really miss your delicate touch, Lord. Would it be possible . . . ?" Walking slowly through the water, I thought, "It's wonderful to have these keys back, Lord, but receiving another kiss is so much better. Thank you for the way you brought this about, for granting my requests, and for a personal reminder of how to ask them."

Postscript

Well, it was Sunday, and I was late for church because I could not find my wallet after searching for an hour inside and outside our property. My greatest asset for finding lost stuff, Emily, was out of town, and I had not heard from Jesus since the boat key caper, so I was done, cooked, and finished. No church today, Lord. No tithe.

Then, in a flash and out of the corner of my eye, I saw a pair of Levi's slung over a chair at the dining room table (hey, I did mention Emily was out of town) where I had been working of late. Relieved, I sighed. "There is the answer; I wore those jeans yesterday. Thank you, Jesus." Scurrying to search those errant Levi's, by their weight alone I knew differently. They held no wallet. Then, disappointed, frustrated, and tired of a brain that ambushed me at every turn, the answer came. How could I have forgotten that principle from Heaven? After all the searching, I had again not been specific in my request. Such a slow learner.

So, without moving an inch, I cried out, "Lord, you know the location of that wallet, and I certainly do not. Please show me." Finishing that sentence in desperation, I glanced over my left shoulder at the captain's chair at the head of the table. There, standing bolt upright and braced like a good Marine against its backrest, in plain sight, and itching to go to church was that wayward wallet. Right away, that sight took me to those boat keys. You too?

Oh, the joy again, not so much for finding the "lost" wallet as knowing, above all things, Jesus was still aware of each step and every breath. So, what could I say except, "Thank you, Lord, once again for exquisitely answered prayer, one more unmerited, undeserved, and unearned Kiss from Heaven, and your touch I have been so desperately missing."

Wallet in place but late for the service, I walked headlong into the church sanctuary and a praise chorus* crying for the personal presence of the Lord. Oh my, right on top of Him doing so in my dining room at home. Twice encountered, twice blessed, and twice undone. Have you ever been ruined in your dining room and a church service on the same morning with the goodness of God? You will never be the same.

*"Draw Me Close," Kelly Carpenter, from CMS Overlake 2008

QUESTION: Where is the Kiss from Heaven from this God Story?

ANSWER: Maybe it's me, but I so miss the Lord if we go long between visits, which are always Kisses from Heaven. It is a joy to call upon Him when He is near and find Him willing to come. It is so encouraging to have the Lord answer prayer but more blessed to simply encounter His presence as He does. Even as I write this paragraph tonight, He has come to bring tears of joy to fall on my computer keys during this surprise kiss. Oh my, He heard my heart longing for Him again. Thank you, Lord, for your nearness. I miss your presence always.

23

Tribute to Daisy (2011)

Any true dog lover understands this: There is a season of grieving set aside to honor a faithful pooch snatched from us in an untimely way (as if losing a loved one is ever timely), be it following days getting acquainted or years of devoted companionship. Only the heart of God can fix that season because He and He alone can fathom when our souls, early wracked with pain, will be open enough to risk another abiding family relationship with a dog. It was no different for this man. Puggles (a name coined well before today's breeders plagiarized it), my three-year-old pug-beagle mix, had her sweet life snuffed out by a big bully log truck on old Government Road near Dorena, Oregon, back in 1987.

After being seduced by a scruffy, shifty ingrate of a male Maltese terrier with an undisciplined bladder (who, incidentally, I had taken in homeless as an act of mercy) to climb what I had considered an unscalable Everest of a front yard fence erected to keep the pooches from a busy, log-truck-laden highway, sweet Puggles had been crushed beneath one of those heartless behemoth's tires. Descending into that place set aside for the walking dead who stumble aimlessly through an empty abyss that separates one faithful Fido's last kiss and the sweet puppy breath of another's arrival, I knew that journey would take a long, long time.

Three years later, on a day like any other, it was over. My dark dog night of the soul ended. The incessant heartache, the inability to remember Puggles without anguish, and the torrents of tears that would surprise me in the most unlikely moments had stopped. It was now possible to think of my little lost girl without experiencing breathtaking abreactions; rather, she had become a fond memory no longer tethered to my heart with grief but with warmth and love alone. Suddenly, I could scatter her pictures on the living room floor to scan the whole collage with joy, each scene merely evoking another fond memory, no more, no less. Then, I knew I was ready.

Puggles and I had met by scanning the classifieds in a local newspaper. Her mother, a cuddly, one-eyed, half-pug half-beagle mix, belonged to a bouncy family up Fall Creek. Mom, as I recall, had endured four litters in four years. Whether planned or a result of sneaky attacks to her right rear flank (suspect to invasion due to her visual field defect), no one knew. Well, things had not changed when I visited her home. In the six-year interim, Mom had survived another six litters. The entire family said in happy unison those days were over. She was in a safe house at Auntie's place up the Mackenzie River under strict quarantine and house arrest. While the family smiled, my heart hit my shoe.

To replicate my little Puggles dog was now a feat beyond hope. A new brood of pug puppies, offered up by the family to ease my disappointment, offered little solace. Leaving in a funk with enthusiasm quenched, could it be that a new pooch was not in my future? Had I reached closure yet? Did I not release my little girl as I had thought? It was a long drive home.

An Early Christmas

A couple of months later, came a phone call. The number was unfamiliar, but the voice on the other end was not. It belonged to a fourteen-year-old young lady (the same little girl who had been

Puggles' brief caretaker six years before). She had "news" for me: "Mom, who is still at Auntie's, has somehow, and nobody knows how, been snuck up on by this neighborhood scoundrel border collie and, guess what, she's going to have more puppies."

"Nobody knew how? After ten litters?" I silently chuckled. We agreed she would let me know when the pups arrived, and I would have the pick of Mom's last litter. "Right," I chuckled again, "Mom's last litter. Not until Jesus gives her one new eye or the vet removes one old uterus, methinks."

It was December, and the holidays were upon us when came my notification that the litter was just shy of three weeks old. The family invited me to stop by at my leisure. What a sight! Again, eight beautiful and perfect puppies but, this time, not with flat faces like Mom and Puggles, but stubby pointed snouts and signs of Dad's unwelcome but influential intrusion. A mixed breed, they would be one-quarter pug, one-quarter beagle, and one-half border collie. All were white, six with black and two with orange markings. They would grow to look like Welsh Corgis with slightly longer legs, best described, I guess, as "stretch Corgis." Sorry.

Watching awhile, I saw a perky little orange girl crawling over top of her siblings in search of another meal. While struggling after an errant teat, she barked, more like squeaked, in frustration. What spunk and tenacity! "That one," I pointed. "I would like that little girl."

On New Year's Eve came another unexpected call from my new little girl's caregivers. "Mom's milk ran out, and our pug with the other litter just cannot manage all the puppies. Could you come for yours now?" *Now*, I thought, *now*? She is only four weeks old. That means bottle feeding and separation anxiety and constant care and... "Okay, be there as soon as I can," that stranger using my voice again replied without permission.

Beginning the Journey

It was a *fait accompli*, and we were on our way home. Here, sitting in my lap (but able to fit comfortably in my palm), was this tiny little orange and white miniature "fur ball" screaming at the top of her lungs and causing me to wonder at the time if some rogue military jet in full afterburner was making repeated Mach 2 low-level runs over our little Isuzu Trooper weaving its way down the Fall Creek Highway. "How," I wondered, "can so many decibels come from such a tiny piehole?" Gratefully, it was not long before my little charge was fast asleep, exhausted from her traumatic separation but giving me time to think of a name. With Puggles, I exhausted book after book, seeking the exact name to describe her unique looks and personality. After an agonizing week, I came upon the not-so-clever yet unique and now-fabled name, Puggles; it was a done deal. This time, I was determined to get this name game done without all the agony. Let us see. What about a flower? Violet? No. Well then, Rosie? Nah. Uh, Daisy?! Daisy! Good name. And best of all, no agony. Yet.

After a quick Wal-Mart stop, equipped with homogenized milk, rice baby cereal, and a doll's baby bottle, we were soon experiencing our first feeding session with surprising skills and success. With my precious "puppers" fast asleep, her chubby little belly padded by a downy washcloth atop my sternum, I took a quick whiff of her sweet puppy breath, fell in love, and drifted off to a sound sleep as we began what was to be our unexpected but treasured twenty-year journey. And what a journey it was to be.

Memories with Daisy

My original full-length, fifteen-page typed narrative of Daisy's life, crammed with her finest and funniest escapades, written during the entire week following her passage, was a way for me to cope with losing a friend and family member of over two decades. She loved me (and finally Emily, who joined us when she was five) with all her heart, and there was not a day we felt otherwise for her.

Her toothy smiles would greet us late each morning as she loved to sleep past ten o'clock in her later years. Other fond recollections take me back to chilly winter nights in the barely heated Monaco RV with Emily snuggled to my back and Daisy tucked in along my chest and belly. It was the best of all worlds, a heater on either side. Priceless. I have never been sure why the dog lost interest, but eventually, she did. Glad Emily did not. By age seventeen, Daisy had developed an arthritic lower back. She was a long dog and, like Dachshunds, prone to losing control of their rear quarters in later years. The anti-inflammatory medications from the vet gave her gastritis, even though they alleviated much of her arthritic pain. She was less interested in food and lost almost one-half her body weight. Still ambulatory but unstable, we discovered an important fact.

Did you know that wolves selectively eat meat and lack digestive enzymes to survive long-term on vegetation? Returning from a visit with the grandkids to a wolf farm (Wolf Haven International) in Tenino, Washington, after learning that fact, prompted this decision: We would feed Daisy only meat and quit the kibble. So, off to Albertson's deli counter for shaved roast beef we went. Wow, what an enormous difference! The old girl's appetite skyrocketed to two meals per day, she gained weight, her activity went up, her coat thickened, and her depression lifted. Troubles with urinary tract infections disappeared, and for over six months, she thrived.

Becoming a walking paradox after years of near starvation-like feeding with expensive plant-based dog food and table scraps, Daisy instantly began to thrive from her Albertson's new delicacy diet. Then, with Daisy soon off arthritis medication, she quickly became pain-free and minus her stomach problems. With stinky black stools (which can reveal blood in the bowel) that were likely from the meat, a trip to the vet helped alleviate the nagging sense of guilt I could not shake.

A Taste of Things to Come

In April 2011, I had an uncommonly realistic dream. Daisy was in an expansive and lush field where a man with his back toward me was throwing a ball for her to fetch. Somehow, I knew it was Jesus. The ball had been her life. In her earlier years, she constantly carried one around, dropped it repeatedly at your feet, and then backed off to give you room to throw. No distance was too far, and no thicket too thick. Then, she was back in seconds and crouched for her next fetch. If pheasants were latex, Daisy and I would, without question, have been National Field Trial Champions. One Christmas Eve, she went as far as rudely unwrapping one of my little two-year-old granddaughter's presents, a doll with a latex head waiting patiently under the tree for morning. If we placed Daisy's ball (to satisfy our own need of a mental health break) in the kitchen drawer, she would sit for hours staring at that drawer until we caved and returned the ball to her. As she aged, this passion lessened but never died. Even in her last year, she would hobble after a ball short distances, subdue it, and then keep it away from you until she was ready. When her lower back failed and her rear quarters and bowel habits steadily weakened, her ball was still never far away. Over her last months, she could barely stand to relieve herself, so we would change her diapers and chucks pads while bathing her daily or as needed. Her nose, unfortunately, never suffered the same deterioration as her eyes, ears, and rear quarters. Understandably, she became humiliated with her incontinence and its odors. The last weeks of her life, as we would bathe her each morning, she would, without prompting, raise her rear leg to make sure we washed her private parts thoroughly. Her brain, I knew from this and other adaptive behaviors, like walking against the wall to keep her balance, never failed her to the end. Then, her colon became partially obstructed. Routine rectal exams showed no masses or blood, even though she needed us to digitally remove her stool each morning.

Closing in on Heaven

Two nights before she passed, I had an identical dream to the one in early April but with added flourishes. The same man, who I again suspected to be Jesus, was throwing the ball for a sprinting Daisy, who returned it at the same rapid pace. Her tail was as erect as a victory flag, and her hamstring muscles as well-developed as in her prime. Closing the dream, the man, after tossing the ball, walked away. Unlike the earlier episode, he turned, smiled, and waved at me.

This time I saw his face. The next time I came upon that face was months later when we bought Akiana's book of paintings and poetry from a woman in Spokane, Washington. By then Akiana was a famous childhood prodigy due in part to her celebrated portrait of Jesus's face painted when she was eight years old. I had yet to get that news flash. Coming upon that portrait in her book was no major surprise. It merely confirmed Jesus as the man throwing the ball for Daisy to finish my dream months before. Years later, in the movie *Heaven is for Real*, the pastor's little boy, Colton, who had an NDE (near-death experience) during surgery, identified Akiana's portrait, among a myriad presented to him over months by his pastor father, as the Jesus with whom the boy had spoken in Heaven.

Following that second dream, I spoke to Daisy, "We know you love us, little girl, but we also know that Jesus is waiting for you. We release you to go to Him." Early the next morning, I heard her quietly whining and yelping. Glancing at her snoozing on her bed, she was in a dream, twitching, paws running and making those happy sounds of a chase. Then, for the first time in two years, she lifted that old tail to high mast and wagged it silly as if chasing the ball.

Returning to that previous night's dream, I knew what this was all about. While I had encouraged Daisy to let go, Heaven was assuring me we were in momentum. For a full month, Heaven had been ready and waiting for our little orange girl. It was now our time to let go.

Saying Goodbye

The morning of her passing, she was crying out repeatedly and struggling against pain as she tried to move her bowels. Emily woke me to digitally help Daisy pass stool, halt the spasm, and relieve her discomfort. She was exhausted and merely a rag doll as I held and bathed her in the shower. It was the most beautiful Oregon spring day of the new year with the temperature in the seventies. I toweled her down, blow-dried her still lovely coat, and put her in the sun on her blanket for the day.

Emily sat with her and watched as she slept comfortably and went through another series of good dreams, one episode in which, Emily said, she momentarily wagged her tail again. At 5:30 p.m., we arrived at the vet's office. She never woke up. When the vet placed the IV line, I would allow no one else to inject her cocktail. I brought her up in this world and would help her out of it. Then died a large part of me.

Postscript

DAISY WOODWORTH (12/10/1990 – 5/3/2011)

Daisy Woodworth (December 10, 1990, to May 3, 2011), best friend and family of Charles Baxter and Emily Anne Woodworth, went home to be with our Lord on May 3, 2011, at 5:45 p.m. PST. She is survived by both her parent guardians and boatloads of folks to whom she simply brought a lifetime of love, laughter, acceptance, and joy. Jesus has clarified her afterlife will be dedicated to "chasing the ball" until rejoined by her family in His time as a long-awaited Kiss in Heaven.

Christian, do you believe animals enjoy an afterlife? If not, read your Bible and renew your mind (Rom. 12:2). God bless.

QUESTION: Where is the Kiss from Heaven from this God Story?

ANSWER: It took another three years after Daisy the dog passed before we were ready. Friends then asked us to let them pray in our next family member. We gratefully agreed. It took another six months before Peachy came to fill the void in our hearts and a home created by our Daisy's trip to Heaven. She has been with us for over eleven years. We love her beyond measure. Isn't a dog's unconditional love in this present world a daily reminder of how our compassionate Jesus did not leave us abandoned but sent Holy Spirit, our indwelling Kiss from Heaven, and His world of agape love (the kingdom of Heaven) to live within all Christians to experience and pass on the Lord's love without measure to those surrounding us until the day we come face-to-face with our Master. Oh, what a day that will be. And don't forget—our first Kiss in Heaven.

* "What a Day That Will Be," James Hill, 1955.

Afterthoughts

I, Caleb, the storyteller and eyewitness in this book, am concerned that I have not adequately conveyed to my readers an unshakable understanding that Father is unrelenting to reveal His active presence in our lives, to keep us engaged in our relationship with Him and that His inexpressible goodness and kindness is always working to exchange His beauty for the ashes in our lives (Isa. 61:3).

Dear Christian, consider how many opportunities each of us has missed to become part of God's divine works, all because we were distracted and driven by the lures of this world, the subtle whispers of our enemy, or the persistent cravings of our insatiable flesh. Or, as we repeatedly have shown here, by being unaware of the Lord in our midst while failing to seek His intervention. Were we all willing to set aside but a small part of our daily consciousness to become ever-ready watchmen on His wall, waiters at His table, or on-call first responders to His every need, how much more might our lives be of use to bring Father glory and honor due His name by praying to glorify His works among men with God Stories, testimonies, and Kisses from Heaven from our own lives?

Yet, despite our failures, He has committed Himself to us for no valid reason beyond merciful redemption for reconciliation, given His only begotten Son to save us from His own wrath, and then kept a door open to His eternal presence by simply asking His very creation, humankind, to believe in Him as God. For that, this world mocks Him for acting as if He were God, persecutes His children for not approving sin or exalting sinners, and reliably takes vengeance against any person, place, or thing that tries to take away the lofty, self-exalted "final say in all things" that humans so often insist belongs to them alone but never to Him.

So why are we surprised or offended this world overflows with pain when He is ignored as our Comforter, full of lies when He is the Truth-Giver, addictions when He is the Deliverer, wickedness when He is our righteousness, depression when He is the Joy-Giver, peace when He is the Prince of Peace, love when He is the Lover of our Souls, and, sadly, on and on? Ultimately, must we not assign humankind's obstinate fallen nature and corporate unsaved soul as reasons for this sorrowful state?

Still, we can take heart, for there will always be a holy remnant of praying Christians in every setting who believe and long to become a recognized landing zone for His presence, lodging for His Holy Spirit, a vessel to disperse His mercy. When a body of believers, gathering together as the Spirit-filled ecclesia, are hungry to see the lost of this world transformed into saints by His undeserved salvation of grace (unmerited favor), we will see many saved, healed, delivered, and set free from the prison of sin-soaked lives.

And because He will never deny Himself the opportunity to be a good Father (Abba), brotherly Son (Jesus), and companion Friend (Holy Spirit), He does all He can to integrate His life with all humanity willing to receive it while pouring out Kisses from Heaven to convince us to trust Him, to believe His Word, and to prove His gospel by way of those unique, inexplicable, extraordinary, or supernatural testimonies (often God Stories like you have recently digested from this book) to the remainder of humankind.

If you already know Him intimately, then you have had a spiritual encounter with the God of the Universe, understand His marvelous ways, and have gleaned encouragement from this little tome of Kisses from Heaven. If you do not know Him and wish to open your life to His love, intimacy, and wonders, merely ask Jesus, and He will take you into a new way of life by way of a new birth, this time a spiritual one from Heaven. So if you make His way the best decision of your life (to be followed by your first Kiss from Heaven), take time beforehand to understand, believe in your heart, and, finally, confess with faith to the courts of Heaven what you are about to read aloud below.

Dear Father in Heaven, I believe that Jesus is the Son of God and came in loving obedience to take full punishment for all my sins so you, Father, could forgive and welcome me into your family as your child. I believe you raised Jesus from the dead so I, too, might walk in the newness of life according to your promise: "If any man is in Christ, He is a new creature; the old things passed away; behold, new things have come" (2 Cor. 5:17).

So, Father, as I have confessed Jesus as Lord and believe that You raised Him from the dead, I now receive your forgiveness, your Son's salvation, and my new life in the Spirit. Thank you, Father, thank you, Jesus, and thank you, Holy Spirit, in whose names I pray. Amen.

Dear Saint, welcome to the kingdom of Heaven and to the Church of the Living God! So blessed to know and love you with the love of our Lord, who lives within us by His Spirit, through us to fulfill His purposes, and aims to be our best friend and mentor.

In Jesus,
Caleb and Emily

About the Authors

Following earlier years as a Marine aviator stationed aboard the aircraft carrier USS Independence patrolling the Mediterranean Sea, participating in the Vietnam conflict, and as a flight surgeon for the US Fighter Weapons School (Top Gun) in Miramar, California, C.B. "Caleb" Woodworth went on to serve as a general and emergency physician in small-town Oregon and later as award-winning Director of the Eugene Department of Veterans Affairs Clinic.

Including intercessor and medical phlebotomist wife Emily Anne, the couple has ministered over the last twenty-five years as ordained pastors and missionaries in restoration (inner healing) ministry among the nations. Amid struggling addicts seeking new lives in Jesus, the Woodworths presently serve as on-call volunteers with Jimi and Ladonna Waggoner's anointed Crossroads Recovery Ministry in Poplar Bluff, Missouri.

In her free time, Emily, as an intercessor, helps keep those ties that bind among family, friends, and the Church while bringing in the afflicted, wounded, and needy for Holy Spirit's healing care. Moments left over are spent sewing, doing crafts, and living up to her reputation as the neighborhood's "cookie lady."

You will find Caleb's days reliably filled with chronicling the Lord's mysterious ways, working in the couples' Face to Face and Listening Prayer ministries, and caring for gentle Skipper and Pony (elderly equines the couple serves as fellow honored guests on Jerry and Sandra Murphy's Moriah Ranch in Missouri). Then, coaxed by insistent rooster Buc-Buc to a morning's breakfast, followed by feeding Momma Kitty and her ever-burgeoning number of feline progeny, it is time to be eternally nudged to a breakfast of chicken wings (that's correct) by overly loved Princess Peaches n' Cream Barksalot, the family's not-so-gracefully aging mostly Jack Russell terrier whose genes have been gratefully toned down by a competing history of pug and beagle—which must be heralded, at least by us, as an unmerited "Kiss from Heaven" by itself.

Emily and Caleb doubt the Lord could be more gracious or life sweeter in their later years. But, of course, they are open and ready for anything more from their First Love. Be certain of that.

To connect with the authors or place an order for bulk copies, please visit http://www.kissesfromheavenbooks.com.

www.ingramcontent.com/pod-product-compliance
Ingram Content Group UK Ltd.
Pitfield, Milton Keynes, MK11 3LW, UK
UKHW032335131224
452403UK00011B/803